Seven Myths About Work

Green Audit

Green Audit (Wales) Ltd. was founded in 1992 in order to provide independent evaluation of environmental data for the Green movement. The importance of this role has become increasingly apparent in the last ten years, as the official response to environmentally linked threats as diverse as BSE, nuclear pollution, food contamination, destruction of the ozone layer, global warming, and air pollution has been to minimize the dangers and to safeguard the credibility of the industrial system.

The aim of Green Audit is to undertake independent research in these areas and publish the findings as books, articles, and occasional papers. More recently its sphere of interest has extended towards the social and economic causes of environmental problems.

Green Audit has received funding from the Joseph Rowntree Charitable Trust, Wales Anti-Nuclear Alliance, Stop Hinkley Expansion, Mid-Somerset CND, the W. F. Southall Trust, and many individual donors. We are grateful to all supporters without whose help we would not be able to function.

Publications available:

Chris C. Busby, *Low-Level Radiation from the Nuclear Industry: The Biological Consequences* (1992, £2; Welsh version also available).

Chris C. Busby, *Radiation and Cancer in Wales: The Biological Consequences of Low-Level Radiation* (£5, 1994).

Chris C. Busby, *Wings of Death: Nuclear Pollution and Human Health* (£10, 1995)

Molly Scott Cato (ed.), *Nationalism in Wales: Essays by Members of Wales Green Party* (£4, 1996).

Green Audit (ed.), *BSE: A Summary of the Scientific Evidence* (£2, 1996).

Seven Myths About Work

Molly Scott Cato

Green Audit, Aberystwyth • 1996

Published by Green Audit (Wales) Ltd.
38 Queen Street, Aberystwyth, Wales, SY23 1PU
(01970) 611226
email: cato@gn.apc.org

ISBN: 1-897761-13-9

Cataloguing information: Scott Cato, Molly, *Seven Myths about Work*.
Keywords: work, employment, self-employment, JSA, stress, benefit entitlement, homeworking.

Preface

There is so much to say about work. What inspired me to pull together this short book was my belief that much of the unhappiness in modern society is caused by work, or more precisely by work as it has been arranged in the present industrial system.

We live on a beautiful planet whose oceans glint and gleam, whose countryside spreads around us, where there is food in abundance for all and enough land for us all to live and peace and fulfilment. Yet every day the people I pass in the street hurry by with sad, anxious faces. What is their hurry? I would venture that work is at the root of it. Yet work is part of what it is to be human. Finding ways of work that are useful and good is therefore an important challenge for all of us.

There is so much to say about work. I would have liked to write about fathers who only know their children for two weeks a year because of work. Or of children who, once adult, blame their fathers for never having been around, when work was the real villain. I would have liked to have written of the tragedy of workers whose lives revolve around their two weeks each year in the sun. So that 25/26 of their lives are spent in endurance for the remaining 1/26 that brings them joy.

I would have liked to write about what we gain from good work. A sense of confidence in our ability to complete the task. Our satisfaction in working together with others on an important project. The pleasure we find in our work-mates.

But this is a short book, so I have restricted myself to considering seven of the many myths about work that colour our thinking. I have intended to present some facts about work culled from research in diverse fields. If we are to reorganize work so that it works for us we need to see through the ideology of work that has grown up since the Industrial Revolution. The first step is to explode the myths that make up that ideology.

Molly Scott Cato
Aberystwyth, August 1996

Foreword

The culture of work that exists at the moment is pernicious and socially engineered. Quite apart from reflections on the unequal distribution of work (Bertrand Russell's distinction between the work of those who moved heavy objects and those who ordered them to do so) there is the more interesting question of the ultimate utility of specific types of work. Since the 1960s, when I was young and first looking at (though not for) work it has been clear to all that science has freed the human race from the ceaseless toil that was supposed to be the lot of the primitive trying to support body and soul: indeed, this biblical model itself is incorrect. But the philosopher Andre Gorz pointed out to us then (*Farewell to the Working Class*) that the owners of the planet and its riches would not easily accommodate their model to one of the future leisure society toward which I looked hopefully, since such a system would allow too much time to reflect on the unequal distribution of wealth among those equivalently enjoying the leisure.

He was certainly right: Thatcher and her think-tanks destroyed the post-war socialist dream and cleverly used the trade union worker culture to construct the vision of a total work-oriented society that is such a part of our present culture now that it is difficult for most to think outside it. This culture was constructed through the alteration of benefit entitlement, through changing the very language of welfare discourse, through training schemes, through the alteration of the school curriculum, and finally through the specious and divisive market forces doctrines which emphasize competition at the expense of co-operation.

But it is exactly this system of market competition and the expansion of industry, using energy, heating the atmosphere, polluting the biosphere, making worthless and unneccessary products that is the cause of the environmental destruction that threatens us all. This is the Green Party's contribution to the question of work. Full time employment for all will destroy the planet. This obsession with work has to be analysed and its consequences investigated. This is why I am so pleased that Molly Scott Cato, of the Green Party, has written this small book to open the discussion of the purpose of institutionalized work at the end of the twentieth century and to call attention to its consequences.

During the Vietnam War I knew many Americans over here to dodge the draft, to avoid being sent to kill people in Vietnam in an ideological war they did not support. They were brave and honourable men—no one, in this country at least, suggested that they were shirking their responsibility. These days we have the Job Seekers Allowance. Anyone who is unemployed has to take any job offered, whether or not it is destroying the planet, producing garbage, or wasting energy. I would like to see people refusing to work in any job they felt was wrong. I would like to see work-dodgers: honourable and brave people who refuse to continue to feed this monstrous culture. We are at a turning-point in history: if we take the wrong road our history will end. Industrial expansion is the wrong road—unequal sharing is the wrong road—full employment is the wrong road. Read this interesting and important book by Molly Scott Cato, and re-think your position.

Chris Busby
First Coordinator of the Green Committee of 100

Contents

What is truth? says Pilate,
Waits for no answer;
Double your stakes, says the clock
To the ageing dancer;
Double the guard, says Authority
Treble the bars;
Holes in the sky, says the child
Scanning the stars

Louis MacNeice

1

Hi Ho, Hi Ho:
The Myth of the Jolly Worker

The most striking thing about work in the twentieth century is just how much of it there seems to be. In spite of the several millions of unemployed people, who are required to ritually beat their breasts in order to earn their dole payments, the rest of us spend most of our lives with our noses to various grind-stones, barely finding time even to talk to each other or appreciate our surroundings. The other extraordinary aspect is that so few people ever question why we should have to work so hard. When I first came upon the collection *Why Work?* published by the anarchist Freedom Press I was faintly scandalized. But the more I have thought about it the more it seems a question well worth asking. Why do so many people feel so unhappy in their work and yet never question why they should have to do it?

And what about alternative forms of societies that we like to think of as `primitive'? Surely without the benefits of technology and in the inhospitable conditions left to them after the world-wide spread of the white caucasian male they must be working night and day to survive? Anthropologists have found the reverse: long working hours seem to be the product of industrial society. Research has shown that in most hunter-gatherer societies people are not required to work hard.

For example, the Kung! bushmen in the Kalahari desert of Southwest Africa and the Hazda, in a dry rocky region of East Africa work only about 12–20 hours per week. . . The Kung youth do not work regularly until they marry (age 15–20 for women,

20–25 for men), and the aged, blind, and crippled are not only supported but are respected for their technical and ritual skills. Childhood, adolescence, and old age are carefree, at least economically (p. 14).

The contrast between the intensity of work for a US worker and the more leisurely pace of life in a traditional society is also brought out by the following quotation:

While a fairly leisurely year for the United States workers (including a full month of summer vacation) involves about 221 working days, the comparable figure for the Kung! would be 121 days. This is enough to support not only the workers but the 40 per cent of the population that is non-productive.

Of course these bush people do not have the benefits of Western technology: they are sadly bereft of computer games and hamburger bars. But, according to the researchers, they do not live marginally, and starvation and malnutrition are uncommon, even during droughts.

So how can it be that with our superior intellects and our advanced technology we require so many more hours from each member of society per week to ensure our economic survival? Why do people in developed societies in the twentieth century work so hard? The answer to this is the ideology that tells us we must work, that makes the question 'Why work?' so difficult to ask. This is what I refer to as the myth of the jolly worker.

The Religious Origin of the Work Ethic

In modern Western society people work on average more hours than they ever have before. We read that the miners of Thuringia, Germany in the middle ages worked only 35 hours a week; life for a medieval peasant was probably similarly untaxing. Researchers have calculated that 'slash-and-burn' agriculture requires 10–30 hours per week; whereas plough-based agriculture, which was the means of survival of most people in Medieval Europe, requires 30–35 hours per week. While life in the middle ages may have been somewhat brutish and rather short, its nastiness seems likely to have been a *post hoc* construction of later ideologists. In Medieval times nearly half the days of the year were 'holy days' dedicated to some obscure saint or other as an excuse for getting drunk and not working.

In his classic *The Making of the English Working Class* (1963; and in his paper specifically on the issue, 1967), the historian E. P. Thompson describes the difficulties faced by the early capitalists in persuading their employees to turn up for work every day at a set time. It took severe punishments to conquer the peasant's or artisan's attachment to 'Saint Monday': a day spent in bed to recover from the excesses of the weekend or perhaps to drink away the horrors of hell threatened in church on the preceding Sunday. According to Thompson, wool-combers did not work Tuesday or Wednesday either. They lit the stove on Monday (presumably still suffering from hangovers) and then returned on Thursday to think about getting down to work. This only left Friday, and possibly part of Saturday, before the weekend revelling started again.

According to Thompson an industrial work structure required a disciplined workforce. The fear of punishment or starvation was part of the processes of discipline, but for workers to be really effective they needed to feel committed to their work: this required the invention of the ideology of work, which originally had its roots in religion.

This is where the Protestant work ethic identified by the sociologist Max Weber enters the discussion. In the case of the weaving communities studied by Thompson the people were Methodists: it was Methodism, which stressed the value of discipline, hard work and frugality. Capitalists found it much more efficient to turn the labourer into his own slave-driver by inculcating in him an ideology of thankless, unrewarding toil in

3

exchange for a place in heaven. 'They weakened the poor from within, by adding to them the active ingredient of submission; and they fostered within the Methodist Church those elements most suited to make up the psychic component of the work-discipline of which the manufacturers stood most in need.' (Thompson, 1963: 355).

Weber drew a distinction between the Catholic cultures of southern Europe which have a more relaxed attitude towards work, and the Protestant cultures of northern Europe, where work was viewed as a religious duty. He gave this as the reason why the economic system of capitalism developed in northern rather than southern Europe. The Protestant faiths stressed the importance of the 'inner compulsion' or 'calling'. It was believed that labour was a punishment for the original sin of pride: God assigned to each person his or her place and that it was the duty of that person to spend all his or her life and energy working as well as possible in that station, atoning for sin and hopefully earning a place in heaven. The accumulation of wealth was actually viewed as a sign of God's blessing. However, it was immoral to enjoy oneself with this wealth: one could only acquire more and then invest it in further industrial projects.

To illustrate the contrast in attitudes to work we can explore the example of the Irish worker, who shared the more relaxed Catholic attitude. The denigration of Irish workers in the late eighteenth and nineteenth centuries knew no bounds. In spite of the fact that it was mainly Irish labourers who constructed much of the infrastructure to support the Industrial Revolution in England, they were despised and forced to live beyond the pale of Protestant civilization. Many towns and villages have an 'Irish town' nearby where the labourers lived. The viaducts, canals, and railway cuttings are testimony to their hard work, yet they were despised for drinking and enjoying themselves with the proceeds.

In Japan the work ethic is also closely tied to culture and religion. It has been a source of great interest that Japan has become more successfully capitalist than the European countries that invented the system, and much time has been spent trying to work out what it is about Japanese culture that makes it such fertile ground for industrial production and marketing systems. It appears that religion also plays an important role in Japan. According to the Japanese sociologist Sengoku Tomatsu the concept of *Bushido* or the way of the warrior is very like that of the Protestant `calling' in the sense of being a religious dictate about how one should spend one's life. It is interesting that Samuel Smiles's *Self-Help*, that renowned encapsulation of ideas about self-improvement through hard work, sold more than a million copies when it was translated into Japanese in the late nineteenth century.

Japanese codes of honour and the particular morality of the Buddhist Shin sect created the perfect cultural support for capitalism in Japan. The sect valued loyalty and collectivism particularly highly, and scientific interests were also important. These religious ideas were transplanted into the workplace so that the Japanese worker can now be said to view his workplace as `a place for his soul to recreate itself, a place for self-improvement, and a place for spiritual training . . . [the worker] looks for the reason of his being or identity in hard work', according to Tomatsu (Schwenkter, 1995).

So we can identify the source of the ideology of work which dominates modern industrialized economies in religious systems which claimed a divine right to control our behaviour and used fear of supernatural punishment to oblige us to work hard. The Protestant idea of vocation actually required people to accept their calling with joy, as a God-given blessing, whether they were king or dustman. So workers should have accepted their positions and worked with smiles on their faces, contemplating their promised celestial throne. However, it seems unlikely that many of these workers were really very happy about it: for the source of the myth of the jolly worker we must look elsewhere.

US Culture and the Ideology of Work

In tracing the roots of the myth of the jolly worker we should remember that the miners who whistled `hi ho' were not Thuringian miners but the dwarves in Walt Disney's film of Snow White, once that fairy tale had been translated to US cartoon fantasyland. Because the Western culture of excessive work and the jolly worker can be traced to the influence of the United States on European culture.

The hard-working nature of North Americans, and in particular their systems of industrial production, has long been noted by their more relaxed European observers. As early as 1922 Weber identified the origins of modern work discipline:

No special proof is necessary to show that military discipline is the ideal model for the modern capitalist factory . . . With the help of appropriate methods of measurement, the optimum profitability of the individual worker is calculated like that of any material means of production. On the basis of this calculation, the American system of `scientific management' enjoys the greatest triumphs in the rational conditioning and training of work performances. The final consequences are drawn from the mechanization and discipline of the plant, and the psycho-physical apparatus of man is completely adjusted to the demands of the outer world.' (from *Wirtschaft und Gesellschaft*, 1992, in Gerth and Wright Mills, 1948).

It may be significant in the formation of the culture of work in the US that so many of the early immigrants were Protestant extremists, exiled from their own countries because of their extreme religious beliefs. The clean-living, hard-working life-styles of those Protestant communities which survive—whether Amish or Mennonite—are renowned, and this must have been influential in establishing an attitude to work before the less noble aspiration to accumulate wealth arrived.

Although this may have provided a basis for the later development of attitudes to work, the general culture of the United States was created by the mixing of the cultures of all the immigrants who arrived there mainly during the nineteenth and early twentieth centuries. While these people had widely differing religious and cultural backgrounds what they all shared was the determination to succeed and the desperation that drives a person to leave all they know behind. For most, very hard work was simply necessary to ensure survival. But for many the American dream came true. They accumulated wealth and ended their days in comfort and security. This seemed to prove the equation that hard work plus long hours equals financial security that still drives the US today when so many people find that in their lives it is not true.

Of course, the real reason why most early immigrants to the USA became wealthy was because of the boundless wealth of the land available. While the frontier remained open anybody could claim a stake in this bounty, and millions became successful. They credited themselves with achieving this wealth through hard work and so work came to acquire an almost sacred status. The wealth they took from the land in producing the Dustbowl or sucking the oil from beneath the desert was misallocated as the fruit of their own labours. America, with its bounty and its emptiness (except, of course, for the native Americans, who were excluded from the fairy tale) enabled the amplification and strengthening of the Protestant work ethic. The United States became the apotheosis of industrial development, the only surviving superpower, and living proof of the rightness of the capitalist system of production. Its political and economic power has ensured that its culture has come to dominate patterns of thought throughout the world, and at the heart of that culture is the reinforced Protestant work ethic. What else do we mean by 'the American Dream' but the fact that hard work leads to wealth and happiness?

And what about the dwarves of Snow White, the archetypes for the jolly worker? Is it any coincidence that their invention in the fantasy-ridden mind of Walt Disney should have coincided with the Great Depression, the largest ever threat to the American Dream. The Great Depression was the end of the fairy tale: the bounty that nature had bestowed on the continent of America had all been used up. The Dustbowl—nature over-exploited and sucked dry—was a powerful and depressing image of the emptiness of the capitalist ideology for many in the USA. It was at this time that many US writers started to question the ideology of hard work they had grown up with, for example John Steinbeck with his portrayal of hard-working farmers destroyed in *The Grapes of Wrath*. The work of these writers who undermined the North American culture was black-listed out of Hollywood, leaving Walt Disney free to create his fantastical images of US life.

Do We Need the Work Ethic?

Although the compulsion to work hard has its roots in religion, it has now become pervasive in the cultures of most developed societies. Since the religion which underpinned this compulsion now has no importance for most of us it is certainly time that we also challenged the attitudes towards work that it gave rise to. However, we should not forget how many of our politicians, those men and women who are particularly driven by a `calling' to organize our lives for us, still profess to a strong religious faith: Tony Blair is a prominent example. He cites his background in the Methodist Church as an important part of his vision. And Margaret Thatcher, who was won of the jolliest and hardest workers in living memory, has been a regular church attender all her life.

Much of the ideology of Thatcherism could have been drawn from the pages of Samuel Smiles: Norman Tebbitt's comment about getting on your bike to look for work is a notable example.

Norman Lamont's equally tactless comment that 'If it isn't hurting, it isn't working' could also give rise to much speculation about the meaning of work within a modern Tory ideology. And I am sure we are all equally tired of hearing how John Major's father removed his circus tights and sequinned shorts and built up his own business through hard work: selling garden gnomes, was it?

So, in conclusion, what are we to make of the myth of the jolly worker? Should we imagine those Medieval Thuringians, throwing their picks and shovels noncha-lantly across their shoulders and whistling 'Hi Ho, Hi Ho' as off to work they went? This seems improbable. It seems more likely that the natural human condition was to avoid work as much as possible, to chat with friends and family, to make enough effort to subsist, and to only really crank up to full power when danger threatened. The compulsion we face today to do more than this, to spend most of our precious and short lives in working for somebody else, is the product of an ideology. And, as we shall see in the following chapters, it is an ideology that does not serve us very well.

The myth of the jolly worker is the first of the myths about work and in a sense it underlies and supports all the other myths. If we all enjoy work so much why do so many of us play the National Lottery every week with a tiny glimmer of hope that we might have enough money never to have to work again? But ideology, it seems, is more important to us than money. How else do we explain the fact that many Lottery winners declare that their new-found millions will not change them, and that *they will keep their jobs!*

If you are still subject to the myth of the jolly worker ask yourself the question: if you could have enough money for all your material needs to be fulfilled, and you could use your time to develop your interests and to achieve any project you feel passionate about, would you carry on in your job? The myth of the jolly worker tells us that work makes us free, that it is the meaning of our lives. But this was the same message that was wrought in iron over the entrance to Hitler's concentration camps: *Arbeit macht frei.* Imagine yourself on your deathbed and think which of your life's achievements you will remember then: would you want to be surrounded by filing cabinets full of reports or rows of tables and chairs you have built or mended? Or would you want to have your family and friends around you, the people you had shared the joys and sadnesses of your life with? It is your life and it is your choice.

References

Eyer, J. and Sterling, P. (1978), `Stress-related Mortality and Social Organization', *Review of Radical Political Economy*, 9: 1-16.

Gerth, H. H. and Wright Mills, C. (1948), *From Max Weber: Essays in Sociology* (London: Routledge and Kegan Paul).

Schwenkter, W. (1995), `Work and Culture in Early Modern Japan', in P. Gouk (ed.), *Wellsprings of Achievement* (Aldershot: Gower).

Thompson, E. P. (1963), *The Making of the English Working Class* (London: Gollancz).

—— (1967), `Time, Work Discipline and Industrial Capitalism', in *Past and Present*, 38.

2

The Myth of Job Creation

Job creation is one of very few growth sectors within the modern UK economy. But what is it for? Could anybody imagine anything more pernicious than the creation of work? The more you reflect on the concept of `job creation' the more baffling it becomes. In this chapter I would like to explore exactly what is going on when jobs are created, what sorts of job are created, and why.

Why Invent Work?

When you first consider the idea of job creation and detach it from the ideological baggage it has acquired within modern economics it begins to seem very much like the invention of work. So why should it be that the government wants to ensure that people are working? Answering this question only requires a brief consideration of the alternative: gangs of young people, drifting and aimless, resorting to theft and vandalism to amuse themselves. This link between the absence of respectable work and socially unacceptable behaviour has long been made by observers of capitalist society:

So long as there is neither school nor work, mischief fills the empty hours. Many of the transgressions, it is true, are trifling . . . But on occasions, the loafing, the roistering, and the aimless wandering lead the idler into depredations more serious than a mere infraction of police regulations. (The Young Delinquent, 1925)

Lord Scarman's report into the Brixton riots showed that such an understanding persists today:

It is clear that the exuberances of youth requires in Brixton (and in similar inner city areas) imaginative and socially acceptable opportunities for release if it is not to be diverted to criminal ends. It is clear that such opportunities do not at present exist in Brixton to the extent that they ought, particularly given the enforced idleness of many youths through unemployment. The amusement arcades, the unlawful drinking clubs, and, I believe, the criminal classes gain as result. (The Scarman Report, both quoted in Clarke and Crichter, 1985: 4–5).

Perhaps the more frightening prospect of people having enough leisure time to start looking around and questioning the power structures and wealth distribution of the society they live in has also occurred to policy-makers.

The emergence and almost immediate disappearance of the leisure age has been commented on by many sociologists exploring the history of work. The dream of a world without work, or with only a few hours work per week, shared equally between citizens, was first suggested in the late 1950s, once post-war reconstruction was achieved, and the production advantages of technology were becoming apparent. These ideas persisted even into the late 1970s and 1980s, as the following quotations show:

Britain in the 1980s . . . stands trembling on the brink of becoming a 'leisure society'. Our future could be more relaxed, more creative, more enjoyable . . . if only . . . we could shed our obsession with work; if only we could take advantage of the possibilities of new technologies and new methods of production; if only we could break our three hundred year love/hate affair with 'Protestant work ethic'. (Clarke and Crichter, 1985: 1)

Perhaps as modern societies move away from labour-intensive industries and as robots line the assembly lines creating a situation of permanent labour surplus, it is time to leave an ideology of work in the attics of the past. (Littler, 1985: 277)

It is interesting that all these authors see the problems that face us as being in our minds. They naively assume that if we could agree to jettison the ideology of work then we could achieve utopia. But, as will become clear from the discussion of the relationship between work and money in Chapter 5, without work it would be much harder to justify the unequal distribution of wealth in our society. For this reason, and for the fear of people with minds unconstrained by the culture of work, once it is no longer necessary for people to work in order to survive, further reasons must be created for them to work. The cycle of unnecessary consumption followed by unnecessary production, leading to further unnecessary consumption, and mediated by manipulative advertising justifies the need for ever more work.

The reality has been that, far from technology reducing the amount of work we all have to do, modern citizens in developed, industrialized nations are tending to work more hours, and the trend is increasing: in 1994 the average British worker worked nearly two hours more per week than in 1988. In the United Kingdom the restatement of the ideology of work occurred during the neo-Liberal revolution of the 1980s. Some right-wing policy theorists were prepared to spend considerable sums to ensure that everybody could have the joy of a job (Howell, 1991). This glorification of work was presided over by Margaret Thatcher. She explicitly lauded the virtue of hard work, which was particularly hypocritical for somebody who had neatly avoided the need to work herself by marrying a millionaire.

So there is a logic to the creation of jobs. Employment as we know it is necessary as a means of distributing wealth and power, as well as productive effort, and as a way of ensuring that those with less of both these important commodities are distracted from analysis the unfairness of the situation.

Jobs at any Price

It has become an assumption of modern politics that the creation of jobs, any jobs, is one of the most important roles of government. Any planning application is more favourably greeted if those proposing it can show that they will be creating jobs. Many of these projects cause vast environmental destruction. For example, the expansion of Manchester Airport is a serious environmental threat. Yet the planning battle has largely revolved around an argument over how many jobs the expanded airport is likely to create. Any menace, from a nuclear power-station to a factory on a greenfield site, is justified on the basis of the jobs it brings.

The recent decision by the South Korean firm LG (the initials stand for Lucky Goldstar) to choose a site in South Wales for the largest ever investment of foreign capital in Europe has been greeted with universal delight by politicians. We are shown a site of some 250,000 acres of beautiful countryside: the pictures are interspersed with images of neat and orderly rows of women operating huge machines and straining their eyes producing electronic components. And we are supposed to celebrate. This is work that nobody wants to do whose creation will decimate a huge amount of beautiful land. The factory will produce electronic components for TV sets. It is a typical example of international capitalism making profits at the expense of everybody: the workers who will be condemned to the hell of the assembly line; the local people losing their fields; the sad consumers (perhaps the same workers recovering in the evenings) who will watch the TV and be persuaded to buy more pointless products manufactured in similarly inhumane conditions. What is going on? It seems that nobody even bothers to ask what sort of jobs they are, whether they produce anything worth having, or whether anybody wants to do them.

In the world of job creation the watchword is: 'Never mind the quality, feel the width'. The glossy literature from Job Creation agencies offers us images of those lucky people for whom jobs have been created. *The New Directions*, a recent strategy publication from the Development Board for Rural Wales includes a photograph of a worker in front of a huge machine crushing garlic cloves, accompanied by the proud caption 'The lifeblood of new business start-ups is vital.' Perhaps the worker, before being expected to spend seven hours a day in garlic fumes with his hands in series of bone-crushing rollers, had been sent on one of their 'Getting into Business' training courses. More likely he had given up struggling after his tenth Jobstart interview.

In Wales the development agencies boast of their success in attracting 'inward investment' to create jobs for our many unemployed people. But what sort of jobs are actually being created? Very often they are the most menial and most poorly paid. A spokesman for LG said that low wages were a factor; the official line was that access to European markets was the main consideration. But since other sites all over Europe were competing (many in countries where employees are protected against exploitation by the EU Social Chapter) the spokesman's admission can be taken as proof that low wages were the reason for choosing Wales, along with government incentives of course.

We have figures to support the claim that wages are lower in Wales. According to official figures, gross *male* weekly earnings are only 80 per cent of the UK average. This makes no allowance for women's work—more often part-time and therefore more poorly paid—nor for all the people who work in the black economy. Surveys of home-workers indicate that many work for as little as 50 pence per hour and official jobs in South Wales frequently offer only £1.50 per hour. Within the culture of job creation companies offering this sort of exploitation are idealized, while without the protection of a minimum wage workers are forced to accept them.

The structure of management in many of the factories funded by inward investment is also a subject of concern. Many of the investors—perhaps Japanese or Korean multinationals—bring with them their work culture of unquestioning obedience. Hierarchies are strict: workers are needed to mind machines, not to become involved in management. And it can be a condition of the company building the factory that non-union agreements should be enforced.

Globalization and the International Fight for Jobs

One of the major aims of the job creators, and of the government departments responsible for paying for the creation of work, is to attract 'inward investment'. This phrase has also taken on an almost sacred ring, so that you feel rather churlish questioning whether these are the same Japanese and South Korean capitalists who are our deadly enemies in the international war of trade. Those companies who provide the much-desired inward investment are the same multinational corporations who exploit workers throughout the developing world, whose power is beyond the control of governments, and whose environmental record is beyond the reach of morality.

In the setting of the global economy we are now competing with workers in Manila or Bogotá. We want multinational companies to create jobs for us and to take jobs away from them. The job creation scam is a fight between workers in different countries attacking each other's livelihoods: the only winners are the managers of the companies which are large enough and rich enough to join in the scam. The workers become ever more powerless: they know that if the workforce is unruly the employers can move the investment to any country where the desperate local people are more pliable.

An important side-effect of this globalization of work is the pointless transportation of consumer items and even of food. Labour costs are an important item in any company's balance-sheet: if it can reduce these costs sufficiently, the additional cost of the fuel to move the products to the markets can be outweighed. This takes no account of the evironmental damage caused by the burning of the fuel: the companies are not required to pay this. A neat solution to this particular dilemma—one advocated by Green Parties throughout the world for several decades—is the imposition of a carbon tax and the removal of taxes on work. The cost of labour to the employer would be reduced, while the cost of fuel would increase. The employer would therefore be more inclined to site his factory near the market, and more jobs would be secured, with less production of greenhouse gases.

Who Gains from the Job Creation Rip-Off

The 1994/5 Annual Report of the Development Board for Rural Wales looks terribly impressive. Leaving aside for a moment the fact that our taxes paid for the four-colour printing and glossy paper, we can marvel at the existence of so many successful businesses in what those of us who live here have always thought of (with relief) as an economic backwater. Fisher Gauge of Canada chose to build their European base in rural Wales; electronic specialists Aerosonic Ltd. expanded to a new factory on Offa's Dyke Business Park; Denis Brinicombe built a new factory for his feed supplements business. Employment is being provided for people in rural Wales. But given the size of the grants involved, can we be surprised at that? LG certainly made a lucky gold-strike.

The more important question is whether these businesses are appropriate to the Welsh setting. Have the people who live in rural Wales been consulted? Do they feel that their futures lie in the manufacture of aeronautical components or animal feeds? Is it their business to have an opinion about these things? As a citizen of rural Wales I, for one, am particularly concerned about the 'New Inward Investment Campaign for Southern Snowdonia'. In the wake of the closure of Trawsfynydd nuclear power-station (what, in a national park?) employment prospects in the surrounding area plummeted. The response was to set up a special campaign and appeal for inward investment.

The advertising copy is appealing: 'Raise your sights to Southern Snowdonia', it beckons, 'the prospects are spectacular'.

Southern Snowdonia now represents a peak of excellence for business and lifestyle. Optimum accommodation for businesses of every type and size, in locations unlike to be replicated, is now available. What's more, a high quality labour force awaits with training and skills highly relevant to safety conscious and procedure led industries.

But do we really want 'businesses of every type and size' in an area of such natural beauty that it is a National Park? Shouldn't more careful consideration be given to the economic development of such a fragile ecosystem? The onward march of job creation seems to ignore such considerations.

One might cynically suggest that one reason the job creators are so assiduous is that if huge amounts of money find their way to rural areas, it will be relatively easy for some of it to trickle off sideways. I am not implying bribery or corruption: those matters we leave to our less developed brethren overseas, but there will certainly be scope for consultancy and expert advice, with attendant costs, when a large investment is made. At a minimum the jobs of the job creators themselves will be safeguarded, perhaps with other perks. According to the DBRW 1994/5 Annual Report the Chairman, David Rowe-Beddoe, received an 'emolument' of £24,870 in 1995. Well, whatever it is, I am sure he deserved it.

Another questionable investment by DBRW was the grant for the development of Aberystwyth Harbour: £600,000. Although I would certainly not write this as fact, it was claimed at the time of the development that an executive of the planning authority was also involved with the developers of the marina. What I can certainly write is that the local people did not want the development. The town council voted against it but was overruled by the district council of Ceredigion, based fifty miles away. The effect for local boat-owners has been a three times increase in the cost of mooring a boat: the facilities provided by the marina are largely unused, and only rich speedboat owners can afford them. Local people have to make do with reduced availability of council moorings.

Perhaps we could justify this in terms of the jobs created. But only two jobs have been created: those of the manager of the marina and his assistant. As a proportion of the grant from DBRW this amounts to £300,000 per job. This is unfair, of course, since it ignores the period of construction. But since this period lasted less than a year, the long-term job creation success of the scheme itself was disastrous. The intention was no doubt partly to encourage wealthy boat-owners to patronize the town's restaurants and shops. In that aim it does not seem to have been very successful either. And any success it might have had would not be welcomed by local residents, who rather enjoy having the town for themselves.

The Cost of a Job

Job Creation agencies, and the government which sponsors them, can be very cagey about exactly how much money is used to persuade companies to set up shop in the peripheral areas of the UK. The recent investment by LG is a prime example. William Hague, Secretary of State for Wales, has resolutely refused to disclose how much was offered to the Korean company, but rumours suggest that it is in the region of £200 million. A report on Radio 4's World at One programme suggested that this worked out at £30,000 per job. As taxpayers we have a right to know that we are buying jobs at such an expensive rate, and also to question whether it is the most useful way for our taxes to be spent.

Speculation aside, we know exactly how much the Development Board for Rural Wales spent in 1994/5, since it is listed in the Annual Report. Leaving aside the assets of the Board in terms of land and other investments (previously provided by the taxpayer) the grants it received in 1995 amounted to £16,289,000. The Annual Report proudly states that `Our target of supporting the creation and maintenance of 1500 jobs was achieved.' It is a relatively simple calculation to divide one of these figures by the other and reach the conclusion that every job maintained or created cost the taxpayer approximately £10,000.

For a worker in rural Wales that represents quite a healthy income. The average male weekly wage in Wales as a whole is some £15,000, and this excludes women, who are traditionally paid less, and workers in the black economy. So it is likely that many of the workers in jobs created by DBRW earn less than £10,000 per annum. But the more pressing and obvious question is: why create the jobs in the first place? The lucky beneficiaries of the created jobs could simply be paid the money directly and allowed to contemplate their navels or develop their skills as landscape painters. They have no need to be poisoned by the solvents used in electronic component manufacture or offended by garlic fumes. Perhaps the garlic crusher at least gains the benefit of some protection against the vampirish economic system that created his job.

The same report on the World at One discovered that different parts of the UK job creation industry are actually competing against each other to attract the multinationals. This is supposed to be overseen by the Invest in Britain Bureau, but this is a watchdog without teeth and the inter-regional competition goes on in spite of it. This means that cunning multinational investors can play one region off against the other, eventually going away with a large amount of our money to subsidize their business and their own high salaries. These are not insignificant amounts of money. The regional aid budget for England has doubled over the past three years and now some 2 per cent of the country's GDP is given as incentives to business. This seems to reverse the trend of taking from the rich and giving to the poor.

Haven't We got Anything Better to Do?

The saddest aspect of job creation is that all the wrong jobs are created. The system is based on attracting inward investment, entangling ourselves more deeply in the growth-based, global economy which is driving us towards planetary destruction. Every new factory, whether funded by Korean, Japanese, or German money, making pointless consumer items to be re-exported overseas, contributes to the environmental damage through its consumption of scarce resources and the fuel used to transport its products to their final market.

The obverse of this unbalanced economy is the huge amount of work crying out to be done in all modern societies. Rather than using our money to persuade Koreans to create jobs making TV components it would be more to the point to spend that money on jobs in social services, to repair some of the social devastation caused by the economic system we suffer from. A more radical and positive possibility would be the creation of a job subsidy scheme, targeted at jobs with environmentally beneficial results. Water companies, for example, could be subsidized to create jobs repairing the leaking pipes which lose so much of the water supply. It is time that the jobs created were the jobs that need doing, rather than the jobs which employer's can use to extract an easy living for themselves.

References

Clarke, J. and Crichter, C. (1985), *The Devil Makes Work* (London: Macmillan).
Development Board for Rural Wales (1995), *Annual Report 1994/5* (Newtown: DBRW).
Howell, R. (1991), *Why Not Work? A Radical Solution to Unemployment* (London: Adam Smith Institute).
Littler, C. R. (ed.) (1985), *The Experience of Work* (Aldershot: Gower).

3

Work is Good for You

Work can Seriously Damage your Health

In 1977 two Canadian medical researchers became concerned at the rising levels of deaths of young people in their society. Although we imagine that life expectancies are improving, much of this improvement is due simply to reductions in infant mortality: Eyer and Sterling found that death rates for adult males were actually increasing. In attempting to understand the reasons for these poorer life expectancies they provided a thorough and fascinating analysis of the stresses of living in modern society and how these might result in deaths from causes as diverse as suicide, murder, accidents, heart disease, cancer, and cirrhosis of the liver.

One of the sources of stress the researchers identified and analysed was work. They paint a vivid picture of the stresses facing a member of the flexible workforce of a developed industrial economy: frequent job change and the related stresses of new environments and social networks; the rapid pace of production and minute division of labour, removing from jobs any interest value or skill; the rapid pace of technological change; the lack of security, in an economic system based on competition between companies and the inevitable failure of many of those companies.

The molding of a flexible fast-paced labor force only begins with the extraction of the worker from communal ties and his subjection to the forces of the market. Faced with the impossibility of satisfying his affiliative impulses, he adapts by steering his tension and frustration into work. The competitive nature of production reinforces the cycle: the harder and more effectively he works, the further he draws away from his co-workers, and the less there is to satisfy him but work itself. (Eyer and Sterling, 1977: 17)

The authors go on to explain how this stress-inducing pattern of work is reinforced by a culture of competitiveness and work that is engendered in all members of society from school onwards. The ideal of an individualist and ambitious worker is established, and those who don't measure up are considered to be personally weak, despite the obvious fact that in a pyramid-shaped employment structure only very few people can succeed in reaching positions at the top. The final stage of the process of 'internal control of the work force' is the translation of natural social and sensual impulses into desires for empty consumer goods, stimulating further production, and further unsatisfied wants.

This chronic, competitive striving, the central adaptation for success under capitalism, is synonymous with chronic stress since it requires and generates constant physiological arousal. This primary adaptation is seen in extreme form in the coronary-prone behaviour pattern described earlier. There are, of course, those who fail to adapt or for whom the cost of adaptation is very high. The cost takes myriad forms: alcoholism (8 million Americans), withdrawal into chronic illness such as ulcer, mental 'illness', and suicide.

This research paper is packed with evidence of the physical effects of the stresses of living in modern society, and particularly of the effects of modern work structures. The data show that movement from agricultural to industrial work structures seriously damages health. The most interesting example is the contrast in patterns of high blood pressure. In urban societies average blood pressure is much higher than in agricultural societies and increases rapidly with age. Indeed, medical textbooks state the increase in mean blood pressure with age as a physiological fact. It is not: in the least developed societies the link between increasing blood pressure and age is absent. Blood pressure levels remain constant throughout life. Since high blood pressure and the diseases it causes—particuarly strokes, heart disease, kidney failure, and others—are amongst the major causes of death in modern society, this is an important finding.

An explanation for the interaction between social structure and stress-related morbidity is given by the contrast in the natural structure of work in undeveloped societies and the closely constrained patterns of work and power relationships in the modern workplace. Bronislaw Malinowski, the founder of social anthropology, wrote about the nature of work for the Trobriand Islanders of the South Pacific (Malinowski, 1921). The structure of work amongst these people seemed well balanced between individual responsibility and work satisfaction and community responsibility and sharing. Thus people were not stressed by excessive responsibility or isolated from others; there was no rigid division of labour leading to tediously repetitive work. All spheres of life: work, social life, learning, celebration were entwined together: this is in complete contrast to the rigidly defined sectors of life in a wage economy.

Some aspects of this type of work structure have survived industrial development, particularly in the agricultural sector. A distinctive feature of life in farming is that it is seasonal and cyclical. There is a varied pace of life throughout the year, fitting in with the natural cycle of the seasons (Newby, 1977). Much of the autumn and winter period is a slack time, as is some of late spring. The very busy times are sowing in February and March and harvesting in July and August. Although work is continuous in these periods, it is also social and workers have a sense of achievement once the period is over, and they do then have a chance to relax. But technological developments have altered this natural pattern of farming. For example, the advent of combine harvesters killed off the annual social ritual of harvest in rural communities. A similar process continues today, and the few remaining social activities are disappearing: for example, hand-hoeing is being replaced by the use of chemical herbicides.

The fact that so many farming families stay on the land in the face of severe financial pressures shows that there is something about the farming life-style that they value highly. The farm-workers interviewed in East Anglia listed the following as being positive aspects of work on the land: variety of work throughout the year; the satisfaction of seeing a process through from beginning to end; the opportunity to exercise skill and judgement; the need to take responsibility and then take the credit for a job well done.

This is in complete contrast to work on the production line in a modern factory. The classic study of work in an industrial system was made by Baldamus (1961) in his analysis of the tedium of repetitive jobs on a production line. He invented the concept of `traction' to describe the `feeling of being pulled along by the inertia inherent in a particular activity.' This was rated as a positive feature, and contrasted with the tedium of the job in general. Baldamus found that workers preferred jobs that were always exactly the same, rather than jobs that involved many separate actions, since they could mentally switch off from the work that was entirely repetitive. Effectively they were extracting themselves from the process and changing themselves into machines for the length of their shifts. Anything which required mental input, such as the change from one small task to another, re-engaged their minds and reminded them of the tedious nature of their work.

To escape the mind-numbing tedium of life on the production line workers are prepared to accept physical pain. Research has suggested that a proportion of occupational accidents are in some sense `deliberate': workers subconsciously injure themselves to escape the boredom of their work (Bynner and Stribley, 1989). Another indication of this need to escape might be the symptoms of chronic disease such as back pain, which can often be neither diagnosed nor treated, and the queues of people in the doctor's surgery on a Monday morning seeking a sick note. Are these workers malingering or suffering from psychosomatic disease? It may not be as easy as we think to distinguish between these two states. One occupational disease even gives its cause within its own name: repetitive strain injury (incapacity of the arms caused by continuous use of a keyboard) has now been accepted as a medical condition, but the research by Eyer and Stirling would suggest that very many of the diseases created by modern society are examples of repetitive strain injuries caused by repetitive, tedious work. As one commentator has remarked:

the oppressiveness of repetitive, pressurised work activities may not result in any dramatic symptoms, only in a slow death of hope in a sea of headaches, backaches and tranquillisers (Littler, 1985: 7).

Work and Leisure

Although the average number of hours worked is increasing, nobody is yet required to spend their entire time working. We have the other side of the coin: the leisure hours in which to unwind and enjoy the fruits of our labours. One aspect of work as structured in modern economies is that it is contrasted very strongly with leisure.

Work is represented as drudgery, approached with a grudging acceptance of that which must be done. It contains little intrinsic *satisfaction and is undertaken to obtain money which allows needs to be satisfied outside work . . . By contrast, leisure seems to offer the prospect of being all those things that work is not: the source of satisfactions, gratifications and pleasures. Where work*

27

is the realm of dull compulsion, leisure represents freedom, choice and creativity. (Clarke and Crichter, 1985: 3)

This rigid division between work and leisure is another product of industrial economies, along with the division of labour and the sexual division of labour. In undeveloped societies work and leisure are more intertwined, with pleasure and social contact found in work. By contrast, in developed economies work seems to be invading the sphere of leisure. According to one researcher, leisure time represented a vacuum that was filled by amusement industries (Roberts, 1981): leisure is no longer an empty space where we can do nothing, but hours which must be filled usefully with `productive leisure'. We might think this implied macramé pot-holders or quilts, but sadly the profit-hungry `service economy' has other interpretations. Pastimes which began as attempts to relax and do very little now become an excuse to sell us more items.

An excellent example is fishing, which I have always thought of as the working man's way of escaping his wife and family. Once upon a time a man would have a cheap fishing rod and reel and would go and sit by the canal; children would make fishing rods from canes and string. But now there are fishing tackle shops specializing in a huge range of different reels, there are a myriad different floats and flies to enable fisherman to catch more fish, more efficiently. Leaving aside the observation that the canal is probably so polluted that there are no fish left in it, this seems to be rather missing the point of leisure. The competitive efficiency ethic has crept into what used to be a reason for doing nothing.

A similar case could even be made about going to the pub. The alehouse of old, with its small range of beers and a few soft drinks, has become another site of commercial enterprise with ever increasing numbers of designer beers and lagers. The art of `cracking on' has died out to be replaced by manic rounds of pub darts or the less traditional jackpot machines and quiz competitions. The only way we can escape the leisure mania is to slump in front of our TV sets: we may be receiving incessant brain stimulation, but at least our bodies are allowed to do nothing. But the age of interactive TV is only just around the corner.

The development of leisure as an industry was no accident. Leisure now accounts for over 25 per cent of consumer spending and is an important sector of the economy. Between 1960 and 1980 employment in leisure services increased by 36 per cent. We cannot be allowed to do nothing, as this would undermine the job security of these people. Margaret Thatcher identified the possibility of productive leisure: in an interview with *The Director* in August 1983 she said `There's a great industry in other people's pleasure'. She was also quoted in the *Daily Mirror* that month as saying `We must expect that a lot more jobs will come from the service industries—from the MacDonalds and Wimpey's, which employ a lot of people, and from the kind of Disneyland they are starting in Corby (*sic*). Leisure is a big industry.' So it is no accident that the art of doing nothing is dying out; it is an economic necessity in an economy with few other opportunities for growth than our precious leisure time.

Work and Welfare

Life for the worker within an industrial economy has been ameliorated since the days of Victorian exploitation. Much has been achieved by organized labour and more recently by Socialist and Social Democratic parties, whose social policies have guaranteed for many workers state-funded health care, free education, pensions, and sickness and maternity benefits, in fact all the necessary components of a modern welfare state. But none of those on the traditional left have challenged the hidden contract citizens are subject to between work and welfare.

The Western welfare state is based on three myths:

- A major aim of government policy is full employment: payments to the unemployed are only temporary while they get themselves back into paid work;
- The family is supported by the male breadwinner, while the woman's role is primarily that of carer and/or housewife.
- Our entitlement to welfare payments is based on our ability to contribute through work, either in the past or in the future.

The first assumption has looked increasingly unlikely in most advanced industrialized countries for two decades or more. The curious thing is that people see this as some sort of tragedy. Much soul-searching now takes place regarding the quest for full employment, as if this were a goal in itself. Nobody ever asks whether some of us wouldn't be a great deal happier not having to. work. The fact is that what people need is not work but money. With adequate money to support themselves most people would refuse the `Macjobs' currently on offer and please themselves. Perhaps they would set up a small business in an area of interest to them, undertake some socially useful but unpaid work, engage in political activism, or simply discuss the meaning of life.

The traditional left have not helped in challenging this particular myth about work. Many old-school socialists are still wedded to the idea of the working man and argue for `jobs for all'. Unions organize marches for jobs and articles abound which come up with generous schemes for buying our way back to full employment or `Putting the Nation Back to Work' (Labour Research, 1995). I wonder why. Unions are wedded to the old ideology of work: is this because they are slow to adapt to changing circumstances or afraid of losing their empire if work loses its central place in our lives?

It is a much more effective and subversive argument to challenge the work ethic itself; this line is also closer to that followed by Marx in his theories of flexible and varied work and leisure. The weakness of the traditional socialist position is evident from its ultimate political weapon: the strike. As a 'working man' the worst you can do is to refuse to work. Of course, this is a powerful weapon, since it makes clear to the exploiting owner the importance of his disregarded worker. But it is ultimately a gesture of weakness, since it is implicitly accepting that the man is essentially only a wage slave and that he only has his labour to make him powerful. The employer knows that without any other power the worker must eventually succumb to exploitation.

The second myth supporting the welfare state is that of the male breadwinner. Ideas about men's and women's different relationships with work are discussed in Chapter 4. In terms of the welfare state, the concentration on the male breadwinner led William Beveridge, the architect of the post-war welfare state, to devise a system of social insurance based on men's contributions. This meant that women needed to stay with men to have the protection of work-related welfare benefits. Many women have been left in penury because they allowed husbands to make NI contributions instead of them and were later abandoned by their husbands. The state felt that it owed them nothing directly, since they had either not worked at all or not contributed insurance payments while working.

The male breadwinner myth has very little basis in contemporary reality. As traditionally male jobs in heavy industries have disappeared, the service sector, providing low-skill and often part-time jobs seen as more suitable for women, has boomed. The movement of women back into the labour force is well documented (see e.g. Joshi and Hinde, 1993). Many families are now supported by a working woman. In other cases to maintain the standard of life considered necessary households need two income-earners. The additional pressure on family members caused by the two-earner set-up can, of course, be catered for by other branches of the consumerist production system: instants meals, household labour-saving devices, increased speed of movement due to cars, as well as provide further job opportunities for those in the service sector.

The crux of the hidden contract between work and welfare is the third myth: the basis of entitlement. From its beginning the welfare state was based on the following contract: `If you work we will support you when you can't work. But if you won't work, you can fend for yourself and the state will not support you.' Marilynne Robinson, an American novelist, has provided a fascinating historical study of British attitudes to social policy as a background for a condemnation of Sellafield. She offers a very harsh judgement of the moral rationale underlying the apparently benevolent welfare state. She traces the roots of benefit entitlement to the Ordinance of Labourers promulgated in 1349 under Edward III. This law required all able-bodied men and women to work for fixed wages: anyone who refused could be gaoled (Robinson, 1989: 47). This particularly harsh Ordinance was a response to the scarcity of labour following the Black Death, but she traces the requirement of work in exchange for welfare to this origin.

A more explicit statement of the contract is given in a law which was passed under King Edward VI, shortly before the passing of the infamous Poor Laws, which held sway until the passing of the equally notorious New Poor Laws in 1834. This early statement of the guiding principle of entitlement to this day makes the contract clear:

that if any man, or woman, able to work should refuse to labour, and live idly for three days, that he, or she, would be branded with a red hot iron on the breast with a letter `V', and should be adjudged the slave, for two years, of any person who should inform against such idler . . . the vagabonds who were unprofitable members, or rather enemies of the commonwealth were punished by death, whipping, imprisonment, and with other corporal pains, it were not without their deserts. (Robinson, 1989: 54-5)

This was the ideological foundation of the first attempts to provide welfare for `paupers'. The New Poor Laws and the system of workhouses which became the ultimate threat to workers in Victorian Britain developed out of the same system, and are based in the same morality. Although punishments have become less harsh the condemnation of the idler remains: `The indigent who were considered worthy of parish assistance were called paupers. The unworthy, those who were considered able-bodied but shiftless, were not to be relieved' (ibid.: 38). Marilynne Robinson writes that William Beveridge himself, as a young man, `urged that starvation be left as a final incentive to industry among the shiftless poor'. The insurance-based social security system he devised was certainly based on self-provision and intended as a scheme for deserving workers on hard times.

This basis of entitlement in willingness to work has now again been made explicit in the Job Seeker's Allowance, which requires evidence of attempts to find work in exchange for benefits, even in areas where it is obvious that no work is available. It is also obvious in proposals for workfare schemes. The rationale for such schemes is the fear of people feeling that that have the right to expect something for nothing. According to the proponent of one such scheme:

The incentive structure would once again encourage personal progress and responsibility instead of entrenching the culture of dependency. Young people in particular would no longer be seduced into the `something for nothing' mentality that can lead them into the worlds of cheating and fraud. (Howell, 1991: 4).

To ensure that we remain compliant workers, when there are no jobs available we must be prepared, in exchange for benefits, to undertake training as a preparation for job opportunities when they do become available in exchange for benefits.

There is an alternative moral view of welfare entitlement: that citizens are entitled to benefits as their share of the national wealth. Particularly in a rich country like the United States, this view emphasizes the immorality of time-related welfare cut-offs for people who cannot find work. What is the justification for leaving people to starve when there is plenty for all? And why should it be that the poor have to work when the rich don't have to? If it is morally justifiable for the Duke of Westminster to live on investment income what is wrong with Joe Bloggs asking for his share of the national wealth to live on?

These considerations lead us to an inevitable and critical conclusion about work. The contract between work and welfare is required to force people to work. The fear is that if money is available as of right, nobody will ever work again. In fact, this seems unlikely, since many people—the foremost example being mothers and housewives—presently work without receiving payment. But what is likely is that nobody would choose to undertake the soul-destroying and mind-numbing type of work required by the profit-driven industrial system, and that those who make profits from this system would lose out. So much for neo-Liberal ideas of freedom when applied to the issue of work.

References

Baldamus, W. (1961), `Tedium and Traction in Industrial Work', in *Efficiency and Effort* (London: Tavistock Publications).

Bynner, J. and Stribley, R. (1989), *Social Research Methods: A Reader* (Milton Keynes: Open University Press).

Clarke, J. and Crichter, C. (1985), *The Devil Makes Work* (London: Macmillan).

Eyer, J. and Sterling, P. (1977), `Stress-Related Mortality and Social Organization', *Review of Radical Political Economy*, 9: 1-16.

Howell, R. (1991), *Why Not Work? A Radical Solution to Unemployment* (London: Adam Smith Institute).

Joshi, H. and Hinde, P. R. A. (1993), `Employment after Childbearing in Post-war Britain: Cohort-study evidence on Contrasts within and across Generations', *European Sociological Review*, 9/3: 203-28.

Labour Research (1995), `Putting the Nation back to Work', *Labour Research*, August 1995.

Littler, C. R. (ed.) (1985), *The Experience of Work* (Aldershot: Gower).

Malinowski, B. (1921), `The Primitive Economics of the Trobriand Islanders', *Economic Journal*, March, pp. 1-16.

Newby, H. (1977), `The Work Situation of the Agricultural Worker', in *The Differential Worker: A Study of Farm Workers in East Anglia* (London: Allen Lane).

Roberts, K. (1981), *Leisure* (London: Longman).

Robinson, M. (1989), *Mother Country* (London: Faber).

4

The Myth of Women's Work

It becomes rapidly obvious to anybody investigating the field of work that it is a discussion largely framed in terms of men's work. The classic Fontana collection of essays on work is actually entitled *Men and Work in Modern Britain*, while most of the essays it contains also focus on the working man. This is peculiar: when it was published in 1973 the movement of women back into the workplace was already well underway.

Women's Removal from the Workforce

Did you notice the way I used the word `back'? It is necessary to stress it because one of the most prevalent myths about women's work is that it is a recent phenomenon. Having previously been trapped at home looking after children women have now been liberated and . . . sent out to work. Since we have already seen that work doesn't make you free, this is a dubious type of liberation. But we also need to explore how it was that women were trapped at home in the first place.

It is generally assumed that the phrase `A woman's place is in the home' is a law of nature that we can now, as a more advanced society, begin to challenge. But in fact it is a myth of relatively short duration. Its emergence can be closely linked to the development of industrial methods of production. Before the Industrial Revolution rather than the woman's place being in the home, everybody's place was in the home. There was no distinction between home and work: in his classic social history *The World we Have Lost* Peter Laslett writes that `the funda-mental characteristic of the world we have lost was that the scene of labour was universally supposed to be the home.' (1983: 13)

This is an important realization when considering women's work, because it meant that all work was shared work. The work was carried out by the family (and this included children as soon as they were old enough to work) and in the family home. The two major productive activities in the UK before the Industrial Revolution were agriculture and textiles and in both women's work was crucially important. In the case of textiles men and women often carried out different parts of the process, but their work was complementary: women spinning and men weaving was a common division. The preparation of wool for weaving was the more time-consuming of the two tasks and it has been estimated that in 1714 roughly eight women and children were employed in textile manufacture for every one man (Oakley, 1976).

What is more, in pre-industrial Britain women were expected to earn their own living and support their own children. Studying list of Old Bailey cases between 1737 and 1800 Ann Oakley found that of the women taken to court only one out of 86 did not have a trade of her own.

Ann Oakley identifies three factors which led to the decline in women's employment:

- The separation of the workplace and the home
- The differentiation of child and adult roles
- The doctrine of domesticity and the creation of a role for the housewife.

The first of these resulted directly from the invention of industrial machines. These were large and expensive and so could not be owned by the craftsfamily in the cottage industry system and could not fit in their cottage. This meant that the scene of work moved to the mill or factory. After the advent of industrial machinery the need for women in textile manufacture declined rapidly; the larger machinery needed men's superior physical strength. Interestingly, it was the men who objected to this, and who rioted in protest at the fact that they would have to support their wives and children.

This also caused a change in the role of the child, who up to that point had been an economic asset and a vital part of the family's productive system. The child now became a dependent, unless employed in the mill. The length of dependency of the child was also extended as education was made compulsory, so the child became more of an economic burden and also needed a carer. This provided a rationale for the woman to stay at home and lose financial independence. While it certainly increased the survival rate of children, it reduced their status, since work had given every child an important economic role from the age of 6 or 7. The ideology to support the ending of child labour was provided by the Victorian chocolate-box images of rosy-cheeked cherubs, contrasted with the unruly demons of the mines or factories. There was matching condemnation of women who 'abandoned' their children to go to work, thus putting further pressure on women to withdraw from the workforce.

Further ideological underpinning was provided by the third factor: the creation of domesticity. In pre-industrial times there was no distinction between home and work: survival was not based on wage-labour and everybody's work . was equally important in ensuring it. But once the place of work was made distinct, and made the man's domain, it was necessary for the domestic sphere to develop its own culture, and to be tended by the woman. The Victorian guardians of morality (usually male) harried women from work on moral grounds: work corrupted the female soul, as was proved by the obscene language and immodest dress of working women; women's health could not stand up to the pressure of work and fertility was particularly affected (curious, then, how the species has survived); working women were also neglecting to tend their exclusive sphere, the newly created haven of domesticity. It is interesting to note the tone of horror in accounts of women with flesh exposed, sweaty, and with large, prominent muscles, and to speculate on its link with the repression and sublimation of sexuality that lay at the heart of Victorian morality.

Feminists have provided interesting interpretations of these male attitudes to women and work. According to Frédérique Apffel-Marglin it is the particular nature of work under capitalism that makes it unsuitable for women. Because women's biological role is to produce babies they cannot be bought and sold in the same way men can: the capitalist labour contract cannot apply to them. Women can only own reproductive labour, leaving the ownership of productive labour to men because in productive labour under capitalism:

The body had to respond no longer to the requirements of performing a completed task done to rhythms set by the household and the wider community, but rather to the abstract epistemized requirements of the industrial mode of production. (Apffel-Marglin, 1996: 152).

Such deep psychological explanations are inevitably speculative while the bald fact remains: during the century of Industrial Revolution many women were effectively removed from the workforce.

Another feature of work in a developed industrial economy is the sexual division of labour. In *Labour and Monopoly Capital* Braverman identified the way in which jobs become identified with one sex or the other. In some cases this is for obvious physical reasons—very few women work as warehouse staff because of the superior physical strength required—but more often it is based on tradition and ideology. Ann Oakley studied two societies living alongside each other in the Congo in Africa. Amongst the Mbuti pygmies of the North-East all work was shared and there was no rigid differentiation of tasks by sex. The society of the Lele of the South-West was completely different: there men and women could not do each other's work. A system of sexual taboos decided who did which work, and men and women could not even walk near each other's crops for fear of spoiling the harvest (Oakley, 1976: 13).

In developed countries the sexual division of labour has become much more pronounced since the Industrial Revolution. Oakley found that in 1574 of 40 smiths registered with the Guild of Smiths in Chester, 5 were women. It was also common for women to take their husband's places as full members of the guild if they became widows. But after industrialization the situation changed and women were excluded from trades. Women's involvement with guilds had ended by the end of the nineteenth century. During the previous century women had worked as surgeons, dentists, and oculists, but with the rise of scientific medicine they were excluded from the professional organizations run by men. The banning of women from the work of midwifery, for which they are surely uniquely well qualified, has been the subject of particular research.

In the modern UK economy most people work in jobs where members of their own sex predominate: this is true for 66 per cent of men and 74 per cent of women. Amongst part-time workers, 84 per cent of women work in female-dominated occupations (defined as occupations with more than 55 per cent of female workers in any year), while only 36 per cent of men work in male-dominated occupations (Hakim, 1993: Table 2). This suggests that women are pushed into ghettos of women's work, and research also shows that wages and promotion prospects in these ghettos are particularly poor.

It has been noted by feminist critics of the labour market that, rather than women being attracted to low-paid work, it may be that once women form the majority of any particular workforce its financial prospects decline. We could see as an example of this the change in the status of secretaries: once a male-dominated profession and the escape of the working class man into the middle class, but later an almost exclusively female job, with poor prospects for promotion. More recently a similar process has occurred amongst compositors. This blue-collar end of the publishing trade was once dominated by grammar-school boys and was a good opportunity for upward social mobility. Since the advent of computer typesetting it is little more than glorified word-processing (Cockburn, 1983). As its status has declined the gender balance has switched from male to female. Another example is found in the so-called caring professions: once women were allowed in the status of these professions declined. This can be seen particularly clearly in Eastern Europe, where the majority of doctors are women, but their status is lower than that of manual workers.

It certainly seems that women's ambition to succeed in the workplace is less than that of men, but much of this can be attributed to social conditioning:

many young women regard work as temporary and unpleasant interlude before marriage and children, which means that they treat one tedious unskilled job as being as good as another. When the myths of romance and ultimate escape dissolve, for many, into the realities of continued work, it is too late. Life has gone by, the chances missed. (Littler, 1985: 3)

A more sophisticated analysis of women's prospects in the labour market suggests that women may be facing a rather stark choice: career or carer. A woman can decide to go for a career and achieve as well as, or nearly as well as, men; or she can have a family and work intermittently and without much chance of achievement. Catherine Hakim (1996) achieved some notoriety recently for her research showing that a certain group of women in the labour force did not want to achieve and that they were bringing down the average achievement for women as a whole. But her point is a valid one: many women recognize that they cannot achieve in the workplace while at the same time bringing up children successfully. They are prepared to make the sacrifice of career to be good parents. It seems a rather harsh choice, when men can always have both work and family, but perhaps it is merely that women have understood more of the mythology of work and have their priorities right.

Invisible Work

When we think about women and work it always seems that some wizardry is going on. Women's work always seems to disappear. From a survey of history it is easy for us to see how little women have achieved: no scientists except Marie Curie (whose personal achievement is somehow always reduced by the fact that she has to be mentioned in the same breath as her husband), few major politicians, no inventors; even in the arts women have had to pretend to be men to be recognized (think of George Eliot and the Brontës). Feminists have explored the way patriarchy operates to exclude women's achievements, and the need to choose between achievement and family has also held women back.

But leaving aside debates about major contributions and the rewriting of herstory, what about the work ordinary women do the world over to ensure survival? Their knowledge of hygiene, nutrition, healing, and basic psychology is essential to the survival of all families, and yet is dismissed in comparison with the more important and male task of being the breadwinner. An interesting example of how this disappearing trick works emerges from research done into fishing on the Indian Ocean coast of Tanzania. A short quotation will suffice to make my point:

Only men's fishing activities are referred to as `fishing',
regardless of whether or not they use boats and nets. Women's
manner of catching fish is not considered `fishing'. Women wade
through shallow waters to entrap schools of small fish (dagaa) in
calico sheets, hence their fishing is referred to by the word
meaning the spreading of the cloth or net, kutanda . . . Women
fish these small dagaa both for consumption and for sale. Dagaa

have become especially popular in recent years as people have found it harder to afford meat and larger fish.

This quotation presents a treat for a discourse analyst: women's work in catching fish is actually defined not to exist. Their manner of fishing is actually called something else, which belittles its obviously substantial contribution to the subsistence of families. Women and children also catch and prepare sea-slugs for sale and collect shellfish and eels for consumption. But these women don't actually *work*, they simply cast pieces of cloth on the water: ah! how quaint!

A Woman's Work is Never Done

I could not resist this particular cliché about work, since it is one of very few that I actually agree with, although it should probably be restricted to women with children. According to the most recent figures I was able to find housewives in the UK work 77 hours per week, while in the US this is 67 hours (Oakley, 1976). Research carried out in 1982 comparing the number of hours worked in the week by men and women found that for all statuses women worked considerably more hours than men. Women who work full-time spend five hours more per week working than do men; amongst part-time workers the discrepancy is even larger, with women working nearly twenty hours more than men. Nor does this allow for the fact that many women work during time included as 'leisure time', since jobs like mending, ironing, polishing, etc. are often done while watching TV or listening to music.

More than just the number of hours worked, it is important that the work that is necessary to keep the household functioning is still culturally designated as the woman's responsibility. This means that women's work is just always there. Even when a woman is relaxing at home she is aware of piles of wet washing lurking upstairs, or dust on the skirting-board. It is in this sense that most women feel that their work is never done, since there is always more work that could be done. In fact many women get to the stage of creating work that isn't even there: a neurotic response to years of conditioning from ever-present chores.

The invisibility of this type of work is what makes it particularly depressing. As a housewife, if you achieve perfection then nobody will notice: invisibility is the mark of success. Let's take as an example the washing of clothes. Because every person you see walking about spruced up to the standard we have come to expect (and how the sight of less white than white people glads my heart!) appears that way because somebody, most likely some woman, has made them that way. Most women are responsible for the washing of clothes for at least one extra person. In my own case I wash clothes for five people. This requires sorting them into white and non-whites, and sifting out woollens or items that need special scrubbing. After washing the clothes must be dried. This generally means pegging them out on a line (especially for we Green types, who shun the tumble-dryer), taking them in and airing them. Then we mustn't forget the constant awareness of the weather that is required to dry clothes out of doors. I have often thought to counter a particularly tedious Force-8 story from a salty sea-faring type with my own personal tale of a daily struggle with the elements to dry my washing.

And then, for those who still believe in it, there is ironing. This can be a lengthy process: up to three to five hours per week. And remember, there are Stepford wives about who actually iron *underwear* and *sheets*! Ironing is one particular chore from which we can easily liberate ourselves. Since most men have never used an iron, if we simply stop ironing standards will be forced to change: creases will once more become culturally acceptable, and the iron can be condemned to the dustbin, or put away for special occasions like funerals and prize-givings.

Most women have given their lives to the mindlessness of domestic work. It is hard to sum up the loneliness and alienation of life at home, probably with children, constantly repeating the same tasks, the highest aim in life being to do all the work so excellently that nobody will notice that it ever needed doing. The life of a woman as housewife and carer is most lovingly portrayed in *The Woman's Room* by Marilyn French. Another description which offers an emotional response to the need to adapt to the status of housewife is provided by S. Gail in a book about experiences of work. She becomes unintentionally pregnant while both she and her partner are studying for PhDs: she decides to do her study part-time, while her partner completes his and then takes a job. She becomes an unwilling housewife:

The housework proved enormously difficult in itself, partly because I was still tired, partly because the place was so large and dilapidated. I was humbled by the discovery that what I had considered work fit only for fools was beyond my capacity. Worst of all, Joe, who had regarded my non-domestication with complete tolerance, suddenly found the dirt and untidiness depressing, and begat status yearning. As a man with a wife, a son and a salary for the uncongenial job foisted on him by Carl's appearance, he wanted a clean shirt every day, not just as something practical, but a his right. (Gail, 1985: 183)

This quotation illustrates perfectly the power of the culture of work to divide the man from the woman and simultaneously to assign to each of them different roles which make both unhappy.

References

Apffel-Marglin, F. (1996), `Rationality, the Body, and the World: From Production to Regeneration', in F. Apffel- Marglin and S. Marglin (eds.), *Decolonizing Knowledge: From Development to Dialogue* (Oxford: Oxford University Press).

Braverman, H. (1974), *Labour and Monopoly Capital* (New York: Monthly Review Press).

Cockburn, C. (1983), 'The Nature of Skill: The Case of the Printers', in *Brothers: Male Dominance and Technological Change* (London: Pluto).

French, M. (1983), *The Woman's Room* (London: Abacus).

Gail, S. (1985), 'The Housewife', in C. R. Littler (ed.), *The Experience of Work* (Aldershot: Gower).

Hakim, C. (1993), 'Segregated and Integrated Occupations: A New Approach to Analysing Social Change', *European Sociological Review*, 9/3: 289-314.

—— (1996), 'Labour-Market and Employment Stability: Rhetoric and Reality on the Sex Differential in Labour-Market Behaviour', *European Sociological Review*, 12/1: 1-31.

Laslett, P. (1983), *The World We Have Lost*, 3rd edn. (London: Methuen).

Oakley, A. (1976), *Housewife: High Value, Low Cost* (Harmondsworth: Penguin).

5

Work Makes you Rich

Since the reason most of us go to work, spending a large proportion of our life doing something we don't like very much, is that we need the money, it is worth exploring more closely the relationship between work and money. The idea that if you work very hard you will become rich and live comfortably is another of the myths about work.

Not Earning but Owning

It is a useful first step to think of people who are prominently and ostentatiously rich and find out where their money came from. We could think of the Queen, the Duke of Westminster, the Sultan of Brunei, or even less exalted examples. It soon becomes clear that the key to being rich is not earning but owning. Most rich people do not work: their income comes directly from rent on property that they own. This property is then passed to their heirs, who become rich in their turn.

An interesting study of land ownership in the UK (Norton-Taylor, 1982), using figures derived from the Royal Commission on the Distribution of Income and Wealth for 1979, found that the top 1% of the population of the UK own 52% of the land. The next 2% own 21.7% of the land. So nearly three-quarters of the land of the UK belongs to just 3% of the population. The same source shows that those with the highest annual incomes own the most land. Individuals with an annual income over £200,000 have 19% of their wealth invested in land. By comparison, those in the £10,000 to £20,000 income bracket have only 1% of their investments in land.

There is considerable pressure to work hard and an implicit assumption is that working hard will ensure financial security, as if there were some sort of straight line relation between work on one axis and money on the other. A moment's reflection will make clear the absurdity of this. As one traditional folk song puts it:

> *Oh, dear me, the world's ill divided;*
> *Them as work's the hardest are the least provided.*

One commentator has suggested that the reason for keeping workers poor is to give them an incentive to work.

The poor, being the producers of this valuable commodity, labor, rather as sheep are of wool, must be kept in an optimum state of productivity. That is, they must be obliged to work in order to live. If they get a little money ahead—this wisdom is often repeated—it goes to drunkenness and rioting. (Robinson, 1989: 67)

So the purpose of the wage structure is to set wages at just the right level to ensure the subsistence of workers, but not to pay them enough for them to be able to stop working.

This is a delicate business: too little pay can lead to rioting or revolution; too much can lead to drunkenness and lack of work discipline. It is as if Alfred the Great's Danegeld, those payments made to prevent the Danish invaders from looting and sacking his kingdom, have become translated into a payment made to the poor workers in wages or benefits—just enough to keep them from following the example of the French revolutionaries and taking by force what they wanted or needed. What becomes obvious is that the system is not set up to allow anybody to become rich through hard work.

The living standards and satisfaction of the worker are not the concern of the employer. This was even true of those who are thought to have had more sympathy with their employees as is illustrated by the work of the early English socialist Robert Owen. Often hailed as a friend of the working man, he describes his method in the introduction to his *New View of Society*: 'which it was my duty and interest so to combine, as that every hand, as well as every spring, lever and wheel, should effectually co-operate to produce the greatest pecuniary gain to the proprietors.'

The ideology that tells us that the route to riches is hard work and keeping your nose clean is really rather misleading, since it is obvious that to be really rich you need to start out being really rich. So it seems that if you want to be rich the best idea is not to work hard but to inherit a lot of money from your parents. What a shame that we have no influence on the accidents of our births. Perhaps it is an indication of the faltering of this myth that the ideology today is that the best way to become rich is to gamble: either the risk-taking of the entrepreneur or the more desperate strategy of the National Lottery.

Flogging a Dead Horse

For the employee the purpose of work is to earn money, but there are also costs involved. Work can become a trap, where in order to begin work you acquire debts or financial obligations, which you then have to keep working to fulfil. If you were ever to stop work then your whole life would collapse, or so it seems. So work is like a treadmill which, once you have walked on to it, you cannot leave without total disaster.

A good example of this is the company shop system that many employers of casual manual workers such as railway navvies used to operate. The worker would be paid in coupons for the company shop: the shop was free to charge whatever prices it wanted, since the workers could not spend their coupons anywhere else. This was the most obvious form of exploitation. But the company shop enmeshed the worker in a more insidious way too. Because the coupons only bought inadequate food for the worker and his family he would ask for credit, which would be willingly granted by the company shop. Now the worker was the victim of the employer, since he owed the employer's shop money and so had to continue working to pay off his debt. He would also have to accept deteriorating conditions and rates of pay.

Another example of this sort of enmeshment is found in a fascinating article about the exploitation of piecework coat-makers in the rag trade on Deeside (Cunnison, 1966). The author describes the system of booking out work to people making waterproof coats which was known as 'dead horse'. 'Under this system the worker is paid at the end of the week for a quantity of work which may include work completed, work in progress, and work booked out to the worker but not yet started. This last was known as the worker's dead horse. It brought the worker into a debt relationship with the firm which, in a sense, tied him to the firm.'

The workers in the factory studied could not decide how much work they were allocated, and so had no control over their earnings. At slack times they did not earn enough to survive, and presumably took on debts outside the factory. But when there was plenty of work about they were allocated work that they could not possibly complete that week, but for which they were paid. They were therefore bound to continue to work at the factory. Since these people were living on the margin anyway, they presumably spent the extra money they were given (or used it to pay off other debts), and then had to take on more dead horse in future to pay their current living expenses. The only way to leave the firm would be to take a week without wages, which for most workers would presumably mean a week without food.

At the factory studied money was also loaned to workers, who were thus more entangled with the company. The author concluded that 'the dead-horse system had two main effects on the struggle over the wage: it put power into the hands of management, the creditor in the debt relation; and it was a source of cleavage between workers.' She gives an example of the way the system influenced the power relation between employer and worker, which is worth quoting at length:

Dead horse also enables the manager to discriminate between workers as regards type of work. Workers with a big dead horse were, in a sense, tied to the firm; and the manager was believed to exploit this by giving them bad work, thus creating a vicious circle of debt. For example, there was Joe: he was a highly skilled long-service maker, but he had a big dead horse and a permanent sub. He had been given an intricate coat which he disliked; it was new and difficult and put him further behind with his work . . . `If I refuse to make them', Joe said, `it will mean another quarrel with Ted Jones. We already had words last week and you can't afford to quarrel with him every week.' Indeed, with a large dead horse and a permanent sub, it did not seem advisable. (Cunnison, 1966: 91)

These stories of financial enmeshment in factories in the 1960s may seem far away from our own experiences of work. But the process seems to be more or less the same today. Once we start work we take on financial commitments. During the 1980s most people in work were encouraged to take out mortgages. The monthly mortgage payment is a sizeable chunk of money every month, and it cannot be varied during hard times. It is therefore a very inflexible financial commitment. It certainly puts considerable pressure on the mortgage-holder to hang on to his or her job. As unemployment increased in the later 1980s and early 1990s many people learned how inflexible mortgage companies could be, as millions of homes were repossessed after six months of arrears had accrued. Many of these people had been persuaded to buy their own council houses and could not adapt to a system of monthly payments which were not only higher than their earlier rents, but could also increase as the interest rate increased.

A lesson learned from this is that if you are in employment you do your best to keep your job. The alternative of financial ruin and homelessness was a real one and the message was clear. Was it a coincidence that the period of increasing home-ownership and consequent well-publicized repossession was also a period of wage freezes and control of union activity? These are really just different aspects of the same strategy of reducing the freedom of the worker.

And for the salariat there are now ever more demands on their earnings. As the welfare state is dismantled, those who can afford to, provide for their own by paying for private health care, private education, and private pensions. On the one hand this saves the government money, on the other it enmeshes the employee in more financial commitments, reducing his room for manoeuvre and subduing his or her protest at longer working hours, lower earnings, and more pressure due to `down-sizing' of workforces.

Work Makes Who Rich?

As long ago as 1867 Marx came up with an explanation of the system of wage work that seem much more convincing than the idea of it as a route to riches. His theory has been called the `surplus value hypothesis', but the idea is very simple. Marx's ideas are based around the existence of two classes: workers and owners. Although today some owners may be pensions funds, in which we all have a stake, there still exist many people who live on share income and have no need to work, so the division is still a relevant one in discussions of work. Since one class works and the other does not, it is obvious that the working class cannot be enjoying all the benefits of its productive work. A proportion of the value of the workers' work is creamed off by the owners to provide their own income.

If we accept this theory then we can see that the amount of wealth we can accrue really depends on a decision about how much of our earnings can be taken by the owners. This is a function of various factors: the ability of workers to find other means of subsistence, the solidarity and organization of the workforce, and the strength of the ideology impelling people to carry on working. Because these factors increased during the early years of this century, owners were forced to increase the proportion of the product that went to workers.

But in recent years all three of these factors have been deliberately suppressed. The ability of people to survive outside the employment system has been declining since the abolition of common land from the seventeenth century onwards. More recently this process has advanced so far that even basic services such as water and sewerage are sold back to us at a profit. People's ability to live independent lives has been reduced by ever-increasing government regulation and local authority planning regulations: witness the difficulties travellers face in even parking their vehicles.

There used to be a space to survive outside the work structure by virtue of the income support system. People who refused to work could survive at the margins of a system really designed for the sick and incapable. But this loophole has been closed with ever stricter eligibility criteria for claimants, culminating in the Job Seeker's Allowance, which requires a frenzy of job searching in return for a measly £35 per week.

One of the most important reasons for the increase in the proportion of the product of labour going to workers was the strength of unions since the end of the nineteenth century. The recent explicit attack on the unions has been carried out through draconian legislation limiting their activities. Less obviously, an ideological war has been waged against unions (Hanson, 1987), who have failed to make much headway in opposing it. But the most effective, and yet indirect, means of destroying labour solidarity has been the destruction of jobs where people work together. The replacement of jobs in the coal and steel industries with `service jobs' where one person sells an article or service to one other person has undermined the power of the worker much more effectively than anti-union legislation. The removal of these jobs has been justified on economic grounds, but the success of Tower Colliery (which was said to be uneconomic but made millions of pounds of profits in its first year as a workers' co-operative) has shown that, at least in the coal industry, this is untrue.

Finally, we come to the issue of ideology: the control of patterns of thought that makes it acceptable to us as a society that owner's returns are constantly increasing while workers face pay freezes. The glorification of the entrepreneur and his right to a limitless income as a hero plays some part here. During the furore over the sizes of salaries paid to the bosses of the privatized utilities, who are operating in the private sector natural monopolies which we all rely on, and therefore can choose the level of their profits, Cedric Browne, the ex-boss of British Gas, justified his telephone number salary on the grounds that he had worked very hard. The relevance of this escapes me. Leaving aside the question of whether a homeworker packing Christmas cards for 50 pence an hour does or does not work hard, why should the fact that he works hard justify him taking large amounts of money from pensioners who need to buy gas to keep warm? The reason he is able to do it is because he has power and they have need, but how can his hours of work represent moral justification?

Another aspect of the ideology of control encouraged by recent governments is the creation of fear. We live in an age of moral panics. This is not to say that awful things do not happen—and as we have seen above issues of crime and issues of work are closely related—but the fact that they are deliberately and salaciously reported by the tabloid newspapers and now by TV news programmes is part of the creation of a culture of fear which makes us all keep our heads down and stick with what we know. As a society we are psychologically intimidated, and this feeds into our behaviour as workers.

Once upon a time work was about making something which was worth money, so that you could sell it for money and use that money to buy the other things you needed to survive. But since the last war there has simply not been the need for this system to continue. We could easily provide for all the needs, at least of the people in this country, with just a few hours work a week each. So it would seem that we should be able to earn enough in a few hours a week to pay for our survival.

But the relationship between money and production has broken down, and with it the relationship between work and financial security. The modern UK economy is based on non-productive income, i.e. income from investments, especially investments in futures, which is the white-collar equivalent of betting on the horses. The major part of the economy today is not involved with production at all: it has no product. So it is not hard to understand why the earnings from genuine products have to be spread more thinly, especially when those who produce least seem to need to earn most.

It begins to seem as if work as established in a modern industrial economy is a structure for justifying an unequal distribution of incomes. After all, if a lone parent with five children has to live on less than £200 per week, while Cedric Browne has something like ten times as much to live on, people might begin to ask questions about the morality of the situation. How convenient that we can scotch any such concern by explaining that Cedric Browne works very hard whereas Marilyn is a feckless poor person who should have listened harder when learning about contraception in school.

It really is time we re-explored the relationship between work and money. We have strayed a very long way from the principle of 'from each according to his ability to each according to his need'. Despite that fact that this maxim is associated with the failed centralised economies of Eastern Europe it still takes some beating as a moral objective of wealth distribution, as some of the new poor of the old Soviet bloc can testify.

Cunnison, S. (1966), `Dead Horse, Debt, and the Wage Nexus in the Garment Industry', *Wages and Work Allocation* (London: Tavistock); repr. in D. Weir (ed.), *Men and Work in Modern Britain* (London: Fontana, 1973).
Hanson, M. (1988), *Taming the Unions: The Thatcher Government's Trade Union Reforms* (London: Adam Smith Institute).
Norton-Taylor, R. (1982), *Whose Land is it Anyway? How Urban Greed Exploits the Land* (Wellingborough: Turnstone Press).
Robinson, M. (1989), *Mother Country* (London: Faber).

6

A Working Life

There is a more or less explicit contract about the relationship between work and our human lives. The deal is that you work from the time you leave school or university until you are anything from 55 upwards. During this working life you put aside contributions towards your pension, and then you retire and, if your health is good, live on the proceeds. This extraordinary idea that you should give all the good years of your life, all the years when you are young and strong, when your body works well, when your children are requiring love and affection, when your mind is active and alive, to somebody else in work, and then finally get around to enjoying yourself when you are 60ish, when your health is failing, when you are an old person, is the most pernicious and saddest of the myths about work.

Saving up for your Retirement

The cruelty of this contract has been noticed by some. Here is what the poet Philip Larkin thought about work in two poems, written eight years apart:

> Why should I let the toad *work*
> Squat on my life?
> Can't I use my wit as a pitchfork
> And drive the brute off?
>
> Six days of the week it soils
> With its sickening poison—
> Just for paying a few bills!
> That's out of proportion

Lots of folk live on their wits:
Lecturers, lispers,
Losels, loblolly-men, louts—
They don't end as paupers;

Lots of folk live up lanes
With fires in a bucket,
Eat windfalls and tinned sardines—
They seem to like it.

Their nippers have got bare feet,
Their unspeakable wives
Are skinny as whippets—and yet
No one actually *starves*.

Ah, were I courageous enough
To shout *Stuff your pension!*
But I know, all too well, that's the stuff
That dreams are made on

For something sufficiently toad-like
Squats in me, too;
Its hunkers are heavy as hard luck,
And cold as snow,

from Philip Larkin, *Toads* (1954)

*   *   *

Walking around in the park
Should feel better than work:
The lake, the sunshine,
The grass to lie on,

. . .

Yet it doesn't suit me,

Being one of the men
You meet of an afternoon:
Palsied old step-takers,
Hare-eyed clerks with the jitters,

. . .

All dodging the toad work
By being stupid or weak.
Think of being them!
Hearing the hours chime,

Watching the bread delivered,
The sun by clouds covered,
The children going home;
Think of being them,

Turning over their failures
By some bed of lobelias,
Nowhere to go but indoors,
No friends but empty chairs—

No give me my in-tray,
My loaf-haired secretary,
My shall-I-keep-the-call-in-Sir:
What else can I answer,

When the lights come on at four
At the end of another year?
Give me your arm, old toad;
Help me down Cemetery Road.

Philip Larkin, *Toads Revisited* (1962)

I think the change of perspective made so clear in these two poems about work is one of the saddest pieces of evidence of the destructive effect of a working life. It is impossible to tell in the second poem whether or not the poet is being ironic as he expresses the security of the life of work, retirement and pension. Did he look back on his utopianism of eight years earlier and scorn it? Or is the poem filled with regret that he was unable to succeed in escaping the 'toad' work. The poignancy is increased by a knowledge of the emotional emptiness of Philip Larkin's life, as childless bachelor and librarian tucked away in a provincial university. I would certainly favour the second interpretation, and I see great sadness and irony in *Toads Revisited*.

For certainly escaping that toad is no easy task. The straight path of the career, with pension and security in old-age as the carrots to lure the donkey along, is much easier to follow. In a developed economy the compliant employee is a necessary part of the machine, and people who would prefer to choose their own path are faced with difficulties. They may be able to survive at the margins of the social security system, but will certainly receive hostility and denigration in gaining their benefits. They will also face social condemnation from people who have accepted the contract. These people, who are wasting their own best years in work, are likely to feel very resentful of others who have escaped the trap and will make them suffer all the pain of social ostracism.

Efficiency and the Work Contract

The system of paid employment, especially with a flexible labour market and disciplined employees, removes from most people the need to use their human ingenuity, to live by their wits. Waiting for a pension is about keeping your nose clean and keeping in with the people who matter, who will provide your pension. If you fall out with your employer you may lose your possibility of security in old age. This risk has become enhanced in recent years, when ageism in employment means that anybody over 35 is coming to the end of their employable life, and that for many positions 45 is the end of the road.

It is neither talent nor intelligence that leads to success in work. In fact being too obviously successful can be dangerous, since it can threaten your superior. The best strategy, once you have accepted the employment contract, is to keep your head down and appear to be working hard. You should try not to make mistakes, and if you do, you should never admit to them, but blame them on somebody else, preferably somebody who has already lost their own job and whose chance of a pension you are not threatening. It is also advisable not to work too hard, or you may show others up and become unpopular with your colleagues. Greater success and promotion is likely to result from spending a few hours each day having a coffee with workmates, and preferably cosying up to superiors.

The nature of the modern employment contract as a sycophant's charter is exacerbated by the introduction of systems of performance-related pay which are becoming more popular in white-collar firms. Since the assessment of an employee's performance is made by his or her superior, the best way to improve your assessment is to ensure your popularity with your boss. If you make a mistake, so long as your boss doesn't know then nothing is lost. And it is more worthwhile to spend some time telling your boss about what you have achieved than actually doing your job.

It is obvious from this discussion of the work contract that the aim for an individual employee is not to achieve his or her best. In this sense the system is grossly inefficient. People who show flair or diligence may well not succeed. But strangely the modern workplace is dominated by the concept of efficiency. Unless a working position can be shown to be necessary in the most obvious and direct sense it is likely to be abolished. The assessment of what is useful is made by management consultants and accountants, so it is no surprise that the jobs which are rarely challenged on grounds of productivity are those of managers and accountants. It would be naive to think that consultants would be immune from special pleading, and they are likely to see their own profession as more useful than others. Evidence for administrative reviews leading to more adminstrators, all of whom claim to be more efficient than the smaller number of them performing the same task in previous years, comes from the reorganization of the National Health Service in the UK.

The quest for efficiency in the workplace has failed to take into account the human aspects of inefficiency. Nobody can afford to take sick leave today because there will be nobody to fill in for them and they will simply have a higher pile of work when they return. So workers go in to work with flu and spread the virus to others workers, and all the workers work below par for several weeks. The same applies to annual leave, where there is very rarely cover for staff while they are away. Employing staff who might cover for absent colleagues would now be considered 'slack in the system' the kind of 'fat' which must be 'pared away' before a company is truly efficient. The extra stress this puts on workers and their consequent reduced morale and enthusiasm cannot be enumerated and so is ignored.

A few sideways perspectives on efficiency might illustrate the point. How often have you phoned an organization during working hours and been put onto a tape of Greensleeves or Vivaldi's Four Seasons? I wonder how many other people put that company several notches down in their estimation and make a note to switch to another one if possible? I am also reminded of a time when I was in an Indian bank waiting for a transfer of money from the UK. As I sweated under the ceiling fans I became increasingly infuriated as the forms were passed from one office-worker to another, the same information being endlessly retyped onto new forms in different manual typewriters. I finally moaned to the friend I was with (an aid worker with some experience of the Indian economy and culture), who replied that if the system worked efficiently there would be much higher levels of unemployment. The final example is drawn from that celebrated bastion of inefficiency the BBC, which is now being sadly pared, tightened and slimmed by government appointees. During the post-war years the BBC provided a home for Louis MacNeice, the Anglo-Irish poet, who was renowned as being remarkably unproductive. But his contribution was immense. Not only in words of wisdom to more productive programme-makers, but also in the volumes of verse he produced during those years. This is certainly a contribution to humanity the BBC can be proud of, although accountants, being unable to value it, would find no place for it in their balance-sheets.

A Lifetime of Work

Some people, contemplating the employment market for the first time in their early 20s, grasp the horror of the employment contract and try to find ways of escape. I have heard many friends in the first years of their working lives outlining schemes of making huge pots of money and then retiring at 30. But how many people do any of us know who have actually succeeded in doing this?

The financial entanglements that follow becoming an employee are outlined in Chapter 5, but there is also a cultural reason why people are very likely to leave employment once they have stepped into the trap. Work takes over your life. The people you meet at work are likely to be the people you spend your spare time with, so leaving your job might well mean losing your friends too. Working for a company, whatever its product, and however absurd or unnecessary, gives you a sense of purpose and meaning in your life. Many people who have become unemployed find the sense of meaninglessness the hardest aspect to cope with.

And alongside this is the lack of structure. Our lives are structured into daily routines from as early as our memories reach. E. P. Thompson considered that this was the main reason for the introduction of compulsory education: children should have their minds disciplined as early as possible to ensure that they could later become disciplined workers (Thompson, 1967). After years of being guided and sometimes controlled in how to think and what to do, suddenly finding yourself with an empty day that it is your responsibility to fill can be very frightening.

The most dangerous justification for walking into the employment trap is the one that says `I will work for a few years and then stop and do what I like.' The danger of this is illustrated by a story about the German artist Albrecht Dürer told to me as an assembly homily at school (it seems likely that the story may be apochryphal, since Dürer wasn't born into poverty, but the point of the story remains valid). The story runs that Albrecht had a brother and that both of the brothers were passionate about becoming artists. They made a pact that one would train to paint while the other worked to support him; then they would swap roles. This way both would receive training and fulfil their potential. Albrecht was to train first, because he was more talented, and he duly worked hard for five years and became the celebrated artist we know of today. But when he went back to his brother to release him from his years of work the brother held out to Albrecht his hands, grown rough and clumsy with years of manual labour. It was obvious that he could never now train those hands to paint with senstivity, that his potential was destroyed. All Albrecht could do was to paint his brother's hands, in the famous painting which is probably familiar to most of us.

The moral of the parable is that waiting for your time to come is a trap. In the context of work the parable tells us that you will not be the same person in five years' time. You will have been changed by the culture of work and you will no longer want to be what *you* want to be today. You will want to be what the firm you work for wants you to be. And you will no longer be able to return to the point you were at and go forward along a different path. The choices you make influence the opportunities available to you in future.

Other people justify their decision to enter the employment contract, perhaps in some cases in highly unethical positions, on the basis that they on their own will be able to make a difference. A person might decide to become a health service manager: she has no admiration for present health service managers but believes that she will be able to increase the value placed on patient care by her own strength of personality. I am also reminded of a young man I once met who decided to work for Shell, a company he knew to be a multinational corporation threatening the future of the planet. He naively believed he could change the direction of the company from the inside. This is rather like using a paddle to turn around a supertanker. One person cannot make that much difference. He or she is much more likely to be swept along in the direction of the firm, and eventually to abandon his or her own views in the face of the pressure of the culture of the firm.

But I enjoy my job, I hear you cry! The power of the human need to justify actions is evident from studies of people in their work. Because it must be said that many people will claim to like their work, and many more feel that their work is valuable and useful, even though they might find the daily grind rather tedious. Some work obviously is valuable and useful, and some work would obviously need to be done in any society: producing food, caring for the sick and elderly, educating the young, repairing streets and pavements and sewers, delivering mail, mending telephones, and so on. The problem is that under the work contract you are obliged to do whatever you do according to somebody else's ideas of what is best. Very few workers are autonomous in their work and so the human spirit is stunted in most positions of paid employment.

An example of this is research carried out on medical students. Most people training as doctors do so because they have an ideal about reducing human suffering. Yet to succeed within the medical profession they need to accept the culture of the profession: for many this comes as a depressing realization that being a doctor is a job like any other. Their vocation to heal and cure has been channelled into another 'job', a production line of sick notes, forms to be filled in, hospital procedures to be followed. Yet very few doctors would admit to this disillusion. Because once in a job we need to justify that what we are doing is right. How many of us have heard friends telling us what a great job they are in, how much they admire the firm they work for, and six months later they resign in disgust for another job, with nothing but abuse for their former employer. But going in to work every day with a knowledge of the awfulness of the work would make it impossible to function, and would also make the danger of dismissal much more likely.

So much for the traditional employment contract. An alternative view of your life might be described by the economics concept of 'discounting the future'. This idea has become more popular amongst so-called economic agents in recent years, as threats of nuclear war and environmental destruction have led some people to question how much future they are likely to enjoy. Discounting the future means valuing more highly satisfactions you can have today than greater potential satisfactions in the future. It is the antidote to the insurance-based view of the world we are encouraged to adopt, where we pay all our money and time over now in exchange for promised paradise in the future. Given that 23 per cent of men and 13 per cent of women die before the age of 65, saving up for a pension may well be money down the drain: discounting the future would certainly have served these people better. Even using the law of averages, a life expectancy of 72 years for men does not allow holders of personal pension plans hope of many years spent in the paradise they have saved for.

The prodigal son is a tremendous example of somebody who discounts the future. He takes his inheritance even before his father has died, spends the proceeds 'in riotous living', as we read, and ends up so poor that he eats the swill given to his own pigs. As a child I could never see the point of this parable. I always sided with the good brother who stayed at home and worked for the father. I always sympathized with his frustration as he saw his father's reaction to the prodigal's return. But it has occurred to me more recently that the father may have been prouder of the prodigal because, paradoxically, he was making something of his life. He was fulfilling his human potential in his own way, and his own growth is demonstrated by his admitting that he could not survive on his own, and his decision to return home to those who loved him.

This interpretation is confirmed by a statement attributed to Jesus in the Gnostic Gospels—some more radical and anti-social pieces of his oeuvre which have been excised from Christian teaching. In the Gospel of Thomas, Jesus is quoted as saying 'If you bring forth that which is within you then that which is within you will save you; but if you do not bring forth that which is within you, then that which is within you will destroy you.' One could imagine such a statement coming from the mouth of Susie Orbach or John Bradshaw or any other modern personal growth guru.

If you adopt the perspective of discounting the future your aim is to make progress in moving along the path to happiness as defined by you. This view is based on a morality which argues that the fulfilment of human potential is the highest aim. If this is our morality then the role of society is to share out amongst its citizens the available wealth and to leave them to decide how to spend their lives. This may seem like a Utopian dream, but a

Basic Income would certainly bring it nearer to realization and allow people more freedom to choose how to spend their short span of life.

It is no accident that the traditional parting gift to a long-serving or long-suffering worker is a gold watch. This is a powerful image of the work contract in a capitalist economy. What you give to the employer is your precious time, most of the precious hours of your life; and in return he gives you a precious time-piece as a memento of that time. You can count off on it the few years of your life that are left to you.

References

Bradshaw, J. (1991), *Homecoming: Reclaiming and Championing your Inner Child* (London: Piatkus).

Eichenbaum, L. and Orbach, S. (1982), *Outside-in Inside-out: Women's Psychology, a Feminist Psychoanalytic Approach* (Harmondsworth: Penguin).

Larkin, P. (1977), *Collected Poems* (London: Faber).

Pagells, E. (1982), *The Gnostic Gospels* (Harmondsworth: Penguin).

Mortality Statistics: Series DH2, no. 19, Table 2 (London: HMSO).

Thompson, E. P. (1967), `Time, Work Discipline and Industrial Capitalism', in *Past and Present*, 38.

7

Working for Yourself

The final myth I would like to address is the myth of self-employment. This is really a myth in two parts: first, the myth of the self-made man; secondly, the myth of the additional freedom for the self-employed, home-based worker.

The Self-Made Man

This myth has been actively propagated by recent Conservative governments. The `small businessman' has been portrayed as the saviour of our failing economy. From the Enterprise Allowance to the teaching of `enterprise' as a subject in school the message is that creating our own work and running our own business is the highest point of achievement within the economy.

The examples that are held up for our admiration are those of people who have successfully built up businesses: two prominent examples are Richard Branson and Anita Roddick. It would be interesting to examine the histories of their businesses in more detail. The tale of Richard Branson—portrayed as a cross between his namesake Whittington and the cheeky Cockney—is a classic example of economic mythology. His business apparently started with him phoning Mike Oldfield from a public callbox to arrange the recording and release of the instrumental album Tubular Bells. This quirky, yet appealing record became the best-selling album of all time and the Branson empire was launched.

So is Richard Branson an example we should all follow? The music industry is one sector where most economic laws do not apply. It is the place in the capitalist economic system where accidents are most likely to happen. Pop stars are often cited as examples of employees whose pay rates do not follow the expected pattern of wage curves. `Intellectual capital' is cited as the explanation, but could surely be challenged in the cases of many of the best paid singing stars. Interestingly, one of these was coincidentally a member of the National Child Development Study Cohort. This study followed all the babies born in a certain week in 1958 to assess how their health and financial prospects might relate to other demographic factors. One of very few of them who had attained millionaire status by the age of 21 was one Gary Numan, lead singer of a successful pop band. The rarity of this is evident from the full sample.

So accidents do happen: some people do strike it lucky and gain success in the lottery of a capitalist economy. Some economists suggest that such people are a necessary occurrence to inspire the rest of us to greater efforts. Because the point to grasp about these rags-to-riches stories is that they are rarities. How many people can produce the best-selling album of all time? It doesn't need a mathematician to figure out that the answer is one. That person is Richard Branson. Since his stroke of luck he has doubtless made wise investment decisions and recognized the value of good PR, but in the world of business nothing succeeds like success.

What about Anita Roddick: `perhaps one of the greatest self-employment success stories in recent years' (Action for Jobs, 1986). Her origins are equally lowly: the daughter of Italian immigrant parents, she started her hugely successful cosmetics business on a £4,000 bank loan. Credit must be given to Roddick for identifying a niche market in eco-friendly cosmetics, and her commitment to Green issues is probably genuine, but in what sense is she a self-made woman? The Body Shop is not a chain, it is a franchise operation. Roddick explains that the reason for this is that she could not finance expansion from the central premises herself, so instead she sold the right to do so to others, taking a fee for the name and the sale of branded products.

Being the owner of a franchise operation is an interesting example of self-employment. A franchisee takes all the risks but only a few of the advantages of the business. As the owner of a franchise business you certainly can feel self-employed and that you are your own master or mistress, but the franchisor always retains the right to withdraw the franchise, and if the overall business is successful, the franchisor will get the glory. On the other hand, if the overall business fails the franchisee stands to lose everything, even if his or her own outfit is very successful. Can this be considered the freedom of self-employment? The example cited in the Action for Jobs brochure (1986) is Carrie, who runs a Body Shop franchise operation in the North of England. Her freedom is rather constrained: 'although she can take time off when she wishes, she usually works six days a week sometimes seven.' The franchise fee for the Body Shop is quite cheap at £3,000; a franchise for a fast food outlet could cost anything up to £350,000.

Richard Branson and Anita Roddick are just two of the mythical figures who are held up as exemplars. They are two of the most prominent examples of the cult of entrepreneurship that has developed under the Conservative governments in power since 1979. It is interesting to consider the concept of entrepreneurship itself, and there is no absence of information, since much research energy has gone into defining exactly what makes a successful entrepreneur. One study profiled eight successful entrepreneurs: the only thing they all seemed to have in common was that they were male (although this aspect was not mentioned: see *The Entrepreneur*). Certainly none seemed to be outstandingly intellectually talented. Another study of *The British Entrepreneur*, prepared by Ernst and Young and the Cranfield School of Management, showed that educational achievement is irrelevant, and in fact suggested that entrepreneurs tend to have demonstrated poor educational achievement (quoted in Jenks, 1991). The study concluded that 'It is dangerous to generalize but some of the characteristics of the entrepreneur, in contrast to the manager, are: belief in himself and his business; belief in wealth and material gain; and belief in delegation.'

We might summarize that what entrepreneurship boils down to is the desire to succeed, the ability to spot chances, and the willingness to exploit them ruthlessly. A capitalist system is based on competition and the entrepreneur is the one who wins the competition. Because if you are successful, then by definition somebody else must be unsuccessful. If you enter a market with a new product, or the same product marketed differently you are certainly only going to succeed by putting somebody else out of business. There are only a limited number of consumers with a limited amount of disposable income. So if you persuade them to buy your product, however wasteful of natural resources or environmentally destructive, or morally dubious, they will not be buying somebody else's product. Understanding and even revelling in this sort of cut-throat competition is what the culture of enterprise is all about.

Many have questioned the morality of this kind of culture. It seems at the opposite pole from Kant's categorical imperative: to succeed as an entrepreneur you must be determined either not to see your competitors suffer, or to enjoy watching their distress as you make inroads into their market share. The ethics of many modern business practices can also be questioned. The most obvious example is the absence of any consideration of environmental destructiveness of products. The response of entrepreneurs to the concern about threats to the planet's future evident at the end of the 1980s was to repackage it and sell it back to consumers. Everything became environmentally friendly, from toilet paper to washing machines, while many Green economists would say that the only environmentally friendly economic future is one where growth stops altogether, or is even reversed.

The unethical nature of many of the activities of the new generation of entrepreneurs has been so questionable that there now seems to be a very thin line between being a swash-buckling entrepreneur and a plain, old-fashioned crook. Perhaps we should replace the word entrepreneur with that more perjorative but more accurate term `privateer'. Should we really be setting such people up as role-models?

The government seems determined to convince us that we all need to follow their illustrious examples. In Wales there is even a programme of social engineering to encourage Welsh speakers to adopt the entrepreneurial route to success. The Menter a Busnes scheme aims to `increase economic activity rates of Welsh speakers by developing enterprise and business as integral creative elements within the Welsh language and culture.' (DBRW, n.d.: 21). This is really just a form of ideological colonialism: hasn't it occurred to anybody at DBRW that the Welsh culture, with its deep-rooted resonances of community and social connectedness, might be inimical to cut-throat compet-ition, and proud to stay that way?

In addition to the ideological onslaught, much government effort and money has been expended in trying to persuade people to start their own businesses. A publication for school leavers under the Action for Jobs (1986) scheme of the Department of Employment encouraged them to go into business. The first case-study business in the brochure is ironically called `Fairy Tales', and is concerned with making wedding dresses. Although the account does mention how hard life is for Dave and Ann—the prince and prince of this particular fairy tale—and informs us that they work from 8 am until 9 pm and sometimes throughout the whole night, the conclusion is an encouraging one:

In spite of their problems and difficulties neither of them have any regrets. Dave says . . . `I Actually enjoy it now. I'd hate to go back to working for somebody else.' He enjoys the responsibility and making the decisions himself. And perhaps the most important thing for Dave is the pride he has in his work.

New small businesses were seen as the solution to unemployment, despite research showing that only 2.3% of those starting up businesses had previously been unemployed (Smeaton, 1992). This was the purpose of the government's Enterprise Allowance Scheme: an offer of £40 per week instead of the dole for one year, and in addition to anything you earned from your own business. In order to enter the scheme you had to invest £1,000: many borrowed this from the bank and then spent it. For some this was simply an opportunity to avoid poverty for a short stretch: business opportunities as fantastical as juggling; songwriting by somebody who could not read music and had never written any; a private detective agency by somebody who had no telephone; or a person who painted decorative horseshoes (according to a personal report) were welcomed onto the Scheme.

The people who viewed the Scheme as a government scam to reduce unemployment figures and cut the spending on dole payments were not too badly off: they ended up with a debt of £1,000 and avoided hassle about looking for work for a period of a year. The really tragic cases were people who took the scheme seriously and borrowed a large amount of money, sometimes using their houses as collateral, in the hope of joining the winners in the entrepreneurial culture. These people, with no real idea about running a business, could easily end up bankrupt and homeless.

The myth of the self-made man is that of an ingenious, intelligent layman who comes up with a good idea, finds a way to market it, and makes a fortune. A coffee-table book of such histories, entitled *How It All Began*, has even been sold to a mass market. We can read of the ingenuity of these model businesspeople, interspersed with tasteful coloured photographs of their quaint packaging, and sepia prints of their Victorian factories. We can witness the construction of the myth of the self-made man: `George Eastman was born in Waterville, New York, in 1854. When George was six years old the family moved to Rochester, and two years later his father died. Due to poverty, George then had to leave school at fourteen and he vowed he would relieve the family of their financial distress.' The heroic George went on to found the Kodak empire. All the stories in the book are based around the accounts of the lives of the founders of the various companies we now recognize as household names. This is clever ideology: the labels we have recognized from childhood, alongside pictures of their founders, and homely stories we can identify with.

But how likely is it that a child finding himself in poverty today could come up with a good idea and set up a business? The cost of development of the sophisticated products we expect today would probably present most would-be entrepreneurs with a brick wall. And breaking into any market requires greater expenditure on advertising than most new businesses can afford. The most likely route is to sell the idea to a larger, established company, swelling their profits and taking a small cut, or more likely a one-off fee.

The reality of life for a person running a small business today is in most cases very different from the mythology that has been created. As Mrs Thatcher was fond of telling us, many of the small businesses are in the euphemistically entitled service sector. Most people would resent being considered as `servants' but somehow being a part of a `service sector' is cause for rejoicing. Much of the service sector consists of businesses selling to us activities we used to do for ourselves but now don't have time to because we are too busy working. This may be the making of food, washing of clothes, cleaning of homes or offices, even car-valeting and telephone-cleaning.

Peel away the glamour of the myth of being a small businessperson in the service sector and you have the dismal reality of owning your own business: hard work and miserable returns. One study showed that while `Popular myth may lead the self-employed to consider the possibility of unlimited earnings', the reality for most was very different. In a cross-sectional sample of people in all employment statuses the richest member was actually an employee. Amongst the quite well off those in self-employment fare better, but `the overall differences between the employed and the self-employed earnings are far from pronounced.' (Smeaton, 1992: 26). The variation of earnings is wide amongst the self-employed, which means that for those who do very well an equal number do very badly. This is, of course, what risk-taking is all about. And even those who have the highest earnings this year have none of the benefits of sick pay, redundancy pay, pensions, and so on, of a person working for a good employer. The self-employed can provide these things for themselves, but are equally likely to invest the money in further growth and to resort to `self-exploitation'.

This becomes evident even when reading an enthusiastic account of small businesses, such as that produced under the auspices of the *Observer* and Touche-Ross, the prominent accountancy firm. This guide to those hoping to start businesses warns of the need for hard work and the risk of financial ruin. (Jenks, 1991). A typical example might be a cafe-owner, working long hours, scrimping on staff to try to reduce costs, ignoring legal standards about rest breaks and conditions of work. Or what about somebody running a small-scale `security services' business? The reality might be an owner forced to employ ex-cons since they are prepared to work for the levels of wages he must offer in order to undercut more reputable businesses. A similar situation faces office cleaning businesses, take-away food shops, local corner food shops. In all cases these are the sectors most likely to pay poverty wages, a situation exacerbated by the abolition of wages councils in August 1993. One study showed that already by November that year, 22.3% of adverts in Jobcentres were offering wages below the previous legal minimums (Cox, 1994).

The Freelance Worker: The Employer's Flexible Friend

One of the most recent myths to be constructed in discussions of employment is the myth of the flexible labour market. This has such a charming ring to it: flexibility sounds so positive. But the reality is the abolition of most of the protection and security of the employee. When in inflexible employment a worker is guaranteed minimum employment conditions: sick and maternity pay; annual leave; pension rights; National Insurance contributions paid by the employer; protection from unfair dismissal; rights to redundancy pay. This is a long and important list: particularly in a context of the reduced role of the state in protection the living conditions of citizens, the loss of these rights and benefits is very serious for most workers.

The other discovery we soon make when investigating the flexible labour market is that it only works 'in one direction. If you are trying to run a small business you find an increasing number of regulations you need to abide by as the government offloads responsibility onto the `private sector', in this case the individual businessman or woman. This has even reached the stage where self-employed workers are expected to compute for themselves the amount of tax they owe the government, with fines for not providing the information to the tax office quickly enough.

The sort of `flexibility' epitomized by the black economy is also being increasingly squeezed. With the government encouraging citizens to spy on their neighbours and report their unofficial activities to the DSS many sideline scams which allowed people to survive while receiving state income support payments are now being made impossible. Life for a small business involves a mass of paperwork and form-filling: very far from the freedom promised by the myth of self-employment.

Many people have been lured off the payroll by promises of greater freedom and control of their own lives: in 1971 there were slightly over two million self-employed people, but this declined through the 1970s to reach 1,900,000 in 1979 (*Social Trends*, 21, 1991). But the arrival of the Thatcher social engineering machine soon reversed this trend. Department of Employment figures show that in 1983 more than 2.1 million people were self-employed and the following year this had risen to 2.6 million (Action for Jobs, 1986); by 1989 some three-and-a-quarter million people were self-employed (*Social Trends*, 21).

But what is the life of the self-employed worker really like? Some trades, such as plumbers or telephone-cleaners do benefit from the advantages of social contact. But the relationship with a client is not the same as the solidarity of others workers which employees enjoy. And for those self-employed workers who work at home and alone, for most of their lives, life is very lonely indeed.

Such lone workers are also very insecure. Very few of the self-employed are unionized (Laurie and Taylor, 1995: Table 4.8), and so they do not have any support in standing up to their employers. Their conditions and rates of pay may be continually reduced: they have no others to compare with and do not feel able to complain for fear of the supposed others waiting to fill their shoes. They do not know their relative skill level or value to the employer. The lone self-employed worker finds herself in an ongoing Prisoner's Dilemma: she has no idea how others in her position will react and can only ever make the most cautious response to any change imposed by the employer.

The scandalous conditions of many home-workers has only recently started emerging, as it has become known that many of the trimmings of the lifestyle of those in secure, well-paid employment are provided by people, mainly women, working in their own homes and for a pittance. According to government figures `Over 3/4 of homeworkers owned their own business or worked on their own account.' (*Social Trends 1996*: 90). Yet the reality of homeworking is far from the life of freedom and autonomy this figure implies. A survey of homeworking in the late 1980s found that those choosing it were not free to choose how or when they worked and that the work invaded their life (Allen and Wolkowitz, 1987). The chapter discussing homeworkers' conditions of work is called 'Mechanisms of Control: The Myth of Autonomy'. One homeworker's account illustrates the stress of having work around the home at all times and fitting paid work around a woman's other forms of work:

I get the kids off to school, then do the washing and clean round for 10 o'clock when the work is delivered. I work through until lunchtime, stop for a sandwich, and continue until 4 in the afternoon. About 6, after tea and clearing it up, I work another hour, get the youngest off to bed, start again about 8 and work until 11 at night. Sometimes I stop work at about 9 and get up early the following morning so it will be ready at 10 in the morning, when the delivery comes. (p. 124)

The rates of pay for this type of work are also abysmally low. According to a recent survey by the National Group on Homeworking the average rate of pay is £1.28 per hour, although most workers are actually paid piece rates. One woman interviewed, Parveen, sews zips into shellsuits, which takes her two hours per suit. For this she receives 40 pence; she works six hours a day and earns between £10 and £15 per week. Another woman sums up the exploitation:

The first time I did these it took me 25 hours to complete. I got £12 and I complained. I'd never worked for less than £1 an hour. He said everyone else is happy. They haven't complained. And you're working at home you know. You should expect less pay. (Huws, 1994: 19)

Of course these women are free to choose not to do this work. But what sort of freedom is it when you know that no other employment is available and that the £15 you earn in a week (the amount lone parents are allowed to earn as a supplement to their benefit payments) will allow you to buy some sweets for your children at the weekend. There is certainly no way of affording even such meagre treats from the money provided by the state.

The most recent development in the area of homeworking—hailed as the means by which the peripheral areas of the national economy can gain from the benefits of growth—is so-called 'telecottageing'. It is rather unfortunate that, in American slang, this phrase implies homosexual prostitution by phone, although not entirely inappropriate, as we shall see. The tele-cottager is the homeworker equipped for the electronic age. Equipped with an email link via telephone and computer he, or more usually she, can receive work electronically and carry it out in the comfort of her own home. Tele-cottageing is expected to become more widespread: a paper from the European Commission in 1994 suggested that there will be 20 million teleworkers in the European Union by the year 2000, many of them working from home (NGH, 1996).

The obvious advantage of teleworking to the employer is that s/he can employ people in depressed areas who are prepared to work for much less per hour. This does open up employment opportunities to those people, but of course it denies others in the metropolis of their chance to earn, or forces them to accept lower wages. So telecottageing could result in a lowering of wage rates to those of the peripheral areas, while workers living in the core of the economy will still have to pay high levels of housing costs and rates.

The heart of the myth of working for yourself is that it implies you are freely choosing what you want to do. The reality is that the self-employed are controlled by the economic system and the need to earn enough money to survive as everybody else is. The truth is that when you are working for money you are never working for yourself.

References

Action for Jobs (1986), *Self-Employment* no. 87 in the `Working in' Series (London: Careers and Occupational Information Centre).

Allen, S. and Wolkowitz, C. (1987), *Homeworking: Myths and Realities* (London: Macmillan).

Maurice Baren, *How it All Began: The Stories Behind Those Famous Names* (Otley: Smith Settle, 1992).

Cox, G. (1994), *After the Safety Net: A Study of Pay Rates in Wages Council Sectors Post Abolition* (London: Low Pay Network).

Development Board for Rural Wales (n.d.), *Jobs Come out of Enterprise* (Newtown: DBRW).

Huws, U. (1994), *Home Truths: Key Results from a National Survey of Homeworkers* (Leeds: National Group on Homeworking).

Jenks, B. (1991), *Small Businesses: How to Succeed and Survive* (London: Hodder and Stoughton, for *Observer* and Touche-Ross).

Laurie, H. and Taylor, M. P. (1995), `Homeworkers in Britain: using BHPS Wave One Data', *Working papers of the ESRC Research Centre on Micro-social Change*, paper 95-3 (Colchester: University of Essex).

National Group on Homeworking (1996), *The Future of Work: Teleworking, the Homework of the Future?*, briefing paper no. 8 (Leeds: National Group on Homeworking).

Smeaton, D. (1992), *Self-Employment: Some Preliminary Findings*, discussion paper no. 96, Centre for Economic Peformance (London: ESRC).

Social Trends 1996 (London: HMSO).

Conclusion: The Future of Work

This is a book without firm conclusions. Its intention is to initiate or continue a dialogue about the nature of work in a post-industrial, sustainable society. To conduct this debate in an informed way we need to have information about people's experience of work. I hope this book has blown away some of the myths that have coloured your thinking about what work is for, and that you will join the debate.

I have already brainstormed many of the ideas in this book in various Green forums: workshops at the Big Green Gathering; fringe meetings at Green Party conference; and various other Green Party meetings. I would like to thank everybody who attended these workshops and shared with others the story of their own working lives. The ingenuity which people have used in avoiding the toad of work has impressed me deeply.

The next stage in the debate is to engage with people who have been told that morality demands that they must work and who still believe this. The Job Seeker's Allowance is helping this debate forward: it is forcing people to explore their attitudes to work and it seems likely that more will ask the question `Why work?' The spread of ecological consciousness is also encouraging many young people to refuse to work within an economic system which is destroying the planet.

There are several ways in which we must take the debate forward:

1. We need to decide as a society which jobs are actually important. I wonder how many people remember the scene from the *Hitchhiker's Guide to the Galaxy* where Arthur Dent realizes that the human race has evolved from the descendents of the spaceship onto which all those with least to offer their society had been packed shortly before their planet exploded. I think they were management consultants, hairdressers, and

telephone sanitizers. Of course, we could all draw up a list of our least favourite occupations. But we do need to do this as a society and to decide what work our economy should focus on. If we decided to abandon manufacturing motor cars this would leave more resources and human effort to keep alive premature babies. We, the citizens, should be making these decisions.

2. We need to talk to people about their experiences of work and analyse these to sift out the bad from the good. This way we could develop systems of work that are humane and make the work that must be done as life-enhancing as possible. Research shows that people are much happier to perform even menial and repetitive tasks if they have social contact and a healthy, happy environment. Worker participation in decision-making also increases the worker's ability to develop as a human being through his or her work. These considerations are just as important as economic efficiency.

3. We need to find ways of sharing the necessary work more fairly; and sharing more fairly the available wealth. A Basic Income scheme, which entitled every citizen (including children) to a subsistence income as of right would reduce the pressure on the very poor to work more, and might also encourage the better off to work fewer hours. The structures of employment that require people above a certain level to work very long hours should also be revised.

4. We need to re-examine the relationship between work and money. In a fair society surely those who performed the most unpleasant tasks would be rewarded most highly, as would those who gained the most emotional feedback from their work. Why should it be that brain surgeons are paid more than cleaning ladies? The wage structure needs to be radically revised according to principles of equity.

So there certainly is plenty for us all to be doing. One thing we can all do as individuals is to withdraw from work as it is organized in today's economy. If we all stopped working tomorrow the system which is destroying the planet would grind to a halt and perhaps our opinions about what work should be like would be given some attention.

That is my Utopian vision. I hope that you, too, will join the debate, because creating jobs for life is a political project with important implications for us all.